Soul Tired
The Price of Holding It All Together When You're Falling Apart

This work is a hybrid of nonfiction and fiction. While it is rooted in actual events and personal experiences, certain elements such as dialogue, character composites, chronology, and specific circumstances have been altered or fictionalized for narrative cohesion and storytelling purposes. These modifications are intended to convey the emotional and thematic truths of experiences depicted. Additionally, names and identifying details have been changed to preserve the privacy of individuals.

Copyright © 2025 Mistrial, LLC
All rights reserved.

Chapter One

I woke to the morning sun, even before my alarm had a chance to go off. The room was quiet, lit with that soft golden hue that only happens in fall, when the world feels still, but not asleep. I stretched, then glanced over at the nightstand.

No pager.

"Damn," I muttered under my breath, rubbing the sleep from my eyes. "Must've left it in the car again." I chuckled, half amused, half annoyed. It wasn't the first time, and hopefully not the wrong time. Around here, a missed call could mean anything from a cat in a tree to a full-blown structure fire. Still, I figured if anything big had gone down, I'd already have gotten a call from dispatch.

I got ready, said goodbye to Sue, she would still be in bed awhile, the boys were sleeping so I let them be and I headed outside. The air was cool, the kind of crisp that bites at your lungs just enough to remind you you're alive. The leaves were halfway through their annual transformation, reds, oranges, and yellows blanketing the trees and already beginning to pile up on lawns and gutters. There was a faint scent of wood smoke in the breeze, the unmistakable signal that fireplaces across town had started crackling again.

My boots crunched against the gravel as I made my way to the car. The driveway was damp from the overnight dew, and the whole neighborhood felt like it was holding its breath. No tourists. No campers. No weekend warriors. Just us locals now. And peace. At least for a little while.

That's one of the perks of living here. Small town. Fewer than 3,000 people. Tucked into the New England mountains, framed by cold, clear lakes and long forgotten roads. It's the kind of town where people wave whether they know you or not and usually, they do.

I've lived and worked here for years. I serve fulltime as a police officer and volunteer for the fire department. That dual role might sound crazy in a city, but out here, it's normal. There aren't many of us, so we wear more than one hat. When the pager goes off, we respond, no matter what uniform we're wearing.

People think chaos only finds the big cities. Shootings, drug overdoses, fiery crashes. But small towns see those things too. The difference is, in the city, you finish your shift and hand it off to the next guy. Here, we don't have that luxury. It's our neighbors, our friends, our families. There's no off switch. You carry it with you.

Some days, that weight gets a little heavier.

I didn't know it yet but today was going to be one of those days, the kind that carves itself into your memory, changes something inside you, and leaves a mark that never really fades.

The road stretched out ahead of me, quiet and still in the pale light of early morning. I kept the radio off. No music, no scanner chatter, just the hum of the tires on asphalt and the occasional whisper of wind through the half open window. It was a cool, peaceful Sunday, the kind you don't take for granted in this line of work. I planned to enjoy every second of it.

My routine was simple. Familiar. After picking up the cruiser, I'd swing by the elementary school, grab the Sunday paper from the box out front, and pull into the side lot. I'd sit there in silence, sipping my coffee and reading through the headlines. Then, when I was done, I'd fold it neatly and return it to the box, just like I always did.

That was the plan this morning.

But as I rounded the last turn before the station, peace was shattered. The town ambulance came screaming toward me, lights flashing, siren splitting the silence like a blade. Right behind it was the paramedic intercept vehicle, meaning they'd already made contact and were now racing toward the hospital.

Nothing had come through dispatch yet, so I assumed it was just a typical medical aid. Still, something about it made my stomach tighten, just a bit. A flicker of unease, there and gone before I could put a name to it.

I pulled into the station, a modest doublewide tucked away on a town owned property, hidden by pine trees and time. It wasn't much to look at, but it was ours.

We're a small department. Just the Chief and me fulltime, backed by four-part timers. No overnight patrols. We respond from home when we're off duty, juggling family dinners and kids' baseball games with whatever call comes next. It's not glamorous, but it's real, and it's ours.

When I first joined, the department was barely functioning. My friend had just stepped in as Chief, inheriting a skeleton crew and a culture of complacency. The former chief, well meaning, old school, had run it like a gentleman's club. Quiet. Passive. Nobody wanted to make waves. But the truth was, our town had become a soft target.

With our secluded roads, central location, and sleepy reputation, we were a hub for drug dealers looking for easy ground. They came here to do business; confident no one would interfere. That didn't sit right with us. So, we made a plan.

We rebuilt from the ground up, shift by shift, hire by hire. We found officers who wanted to be part of something real, something professional. Today, we're that team. No more open-air drug deals. No more quiet look aways. People in town trust us now. They count on us. I took pride in that, deep pride.

I loved the work. The challenge. The variety. I loved knowing I could make a difference, even if it was just one call at a time. I believed in the mission, in the department, in the people. I was all in. I didn't think anything could ever change that.

But that morning was the beginning of a shift I didn't see coming, one I couldn't stop, even when I tried.

I unlocked the deadbolt and stepped inside, the soft chime of the alarm immediately turning into a steady beep. Without thinking, I reached for the keypad and punched in the code, silencing it. Nothing looked out of place. Reid had worked the night shift and, as always, had set the alarm before heading home. Routine. Predictable. Just like any other morning.

I was early, no surprise there. I'm always early. Usually, I'd take this quiet time to set up my cruiser. Make sure my bag was packed right, organize my gear, double check the equipment, then settle at my desk to skim emails, look through previous shifts call logs, and sign in-service on the radio. That was the rhythm. That was the routine.

But today was different.

I hadn't even taken my bag off my shoulder. It was still slung there, heavy and forgotten, as I walked straight to the phone like I was being pulled by something unseen. I didn't know why, just that I had to. A pressure in my chest, sharp and sudden, told me to call before I did anything else. Not a decision. Not a thought. Just instinct. Muscle memory wrapped in dread.

I picked up the receiver and dialed dispatch.

The second the line clicked open, I knew.
Not from the words. Not yet.
From the silence.
From the way the air seemed to hold its breath.

"Oh, thank God," the dispatcher said, breathless. "We've been trying the Chief. He's not answering. You need to get to Reid's house, now."

My whole body went still.

"What's going on?" I asked, though my voice didn't sound like mine.

"All we have is... a suicide attempt."

The words didn't register. Not right away. But then something inside me buckled. My knees locked. My stomach turned inside out. I felt like I was falling while standing perfectly still.

The ambulance I passed earlier. The intercept vehicle I didn't think twice about.
No. No. No.

Please, God, not one of the boys.

Reid isn't just a guy I work with; he's my best friend. I brought him into the department. I trained him. I trusted him with my life more times than I can count. His family is part of mine. Mara, his wife, always made sure there was a place for Sue and me at their table. Their two boys were like nephews to me, laughing, chasing fireflies in the yard while we sat on the porch solving the world's problems over beer and barbecue.

And now this.

When dispatch said, "Reid's house," something deep inside me twisted. My thoughts went straight to the kids. It had to be them. I didn't want it to be, but that's where my head went. Maybe because I've seen it, too many times. Young boys, alone, confused, chasing a high they don't understand. We'd had a string of autoerotic asphyxia cases in the region lately, quiet tragedies where no one saw it coming until it was too late. It's a dangerous act, often involving self-strangulation in pursuit of heightened sensation, risky, secretive, and deadly when something goes wrong. That's what I told myself. In a twisted way that's what I hoped it was.

But the truth was already unravelling. Heartbreak was just beginning its slow, merciless crawl through my chest.

I dropped the phone, just let it fall.

I ran. I must've grabbed the keys, must've opened the cruiser door, but I don't remember any of it. Just the engine roaring. Just the scream of the siren tearing a hole through the stillness of the morning. The world outside blurred into streaks of trees and frost covered mailboxes. My hands gripped the wheel, but they weren't steady.

My heart pounded so hard it drowned out the radio.

I don't remember the turns I took. I don't remember how long it took. I just remember pulling into the cul-de-sac.

The van was already there.

The sliding door hung open like a broken jaw.

Then I saw it,
A black hose snaked through the back window, heavy and deliberate. Lying there like a sentence waiting for a verdict. The van was pulled almost all the way out of the garage, garage door open.

Time stopped.

There was no crowd. No shouting. Just a cold, devastating silence that settled over everything like ash.

    This wasn't just another call,
    This was *my* call,
    This was family.

In that moment, I wasn't a cop. I wasn't a firefighter. I wasn't a responder trained to keep it together.

I was just a man
Staring at the doorway
Of a life that would never be the same again.

As I stood there in the driveway, staring at that black hose curling out of the van window like a snake, everything else around me faded. My breath caught in my throat, and time seemed to slow. In that silence, before I could move, before I could act, my mind took me somewhere else entirely.

Just three nights earlier, we'd all gone out to dinner. Me, Sue, Reid and Mara. One of those casual evenings that felt like a break from everything else, kids, work, sirens. We met at our favorite little place on the edge of town, the kind with the sticky menus and the friendly waitress who never needs to ask for our order. We always sat at the same booth. We always ordered too much, and we always laughed, God, did we laugh that night.

Reid was in rare form, making fun of the awful 80s playlist they had running on repeat. He and I cracked jokes about calls we'd been on together, some funny, some just absurd. Mara rolled her eyes the way only a wife can. My wife told me to stop talking shop and for a little while, everything felt normal. Easy. Like the world was simple and kind and made sense.

If someone had told me that night that three days later, I'd be standing in their driveway, wondering if Reid was dead… I wouldn't have believed it.

But that's the thing no one tells you about this job. The people you protect, the people you serve, it's not always strangers. Sometimes, it's your closest friends. Your brothers. The ones you never imagined you'd have to save.

The laughter from that night echoed in my mind as I stood frozen beside the cruiser, the image of that black hose still burning into my vision. The flash of memory faded, and I was back in the driveway, back in the cold, still morning.

The driveway was still littered with the chaos of emergency response, medical bags, gloves, the van's door still open like a wound that wouldn't close. A couple of firefighters remained on scene, their usual confidence replaced by a quiet stiffness, like they didn't quite know what to do with themselves.

Jack was one of us. A part time cop, a firefighter, and a friend. The kind of guy who always had your back, no matter what. He was already outside when I pulled up, standing stiff in the driveway, arms crossed like he was trying to hold himself together.

When he saw me, he started walking over fast.

His face stopped me cold.

He looked pale, like all the color had drained out of him. His eyes were glassy, unfocused, and full of something I couldn't name but felt like grief. Not panic. Not adrenaline. Just... devastation.

That told me everything before he even opened his mouth.

"It's Mara," he said quietly, barely above a whisper. Like her name might break apart if he said it too loud.

I blinked, trying to process. "Mara?" I repeated, dumbfounded. "Mara was in the van?"

That wasn't possible. Couldn't be.

Of all the horrible scenarios I had imagined on the way over, all the chaos my brain had spun up in seconds, Mara wasn't even in the running. Not once. Not even close.

She wasn't supposed to be the one.

Not Mara. Not the woman who lit up every room. Not the mom who laughed loudest at her kids' jokes. Not the friend who always made sure Sue had someone to talk to when the job swallowed me whole.

Not the steady, bright soul we all leaned on without even realizing we were doing it.

Now… she was the one in the van?

I felt something deep in my chest snap. Quietly. Cleanly. Like a wire stretched too tight, finally giving way.

The world tilted. My thoughts scattered.

This wasn't just grief. This was confusion crashing headfirst into disbelief and losing.

He nodded. "Yeah… Reid's gone with the ambulance. They were working her when they left."

That was actually good to hear, "working her" means there was sign of life, they were doing lifesaving actions, whatever was needed.

I didn't even realize I was holding my breath until Jack touched my shoulder.

"She wasn't responsive," he said. "But they were trying everything. Reid rode in with her."

I walked over to the van, instinct kicking in like muscle memory, part cop, part firefighter, part friend. I slipped into investigator mode, because it was the only thing keeping me from falling apart.

The black hose wasn't in the exhaust like I'd feared. Instead, it snaked in through a slightly cracked rear window, just wide enough to thread it inside. My eyes scanned the interior. There were articles of clothing strewn about, the kinds of things you'd expect in a van that belongs to a family with three young boys, sweatshirts, a soccer cleat, fast food wrappers, crumpled drawings from school. The middle bench seat was reclined slightly, like someone had laid back to rest. On the floor, a massage gun with its chord snaked up to the front cigarette lighter for power. More clutter. More innocence.

It hit me like a punch to the chest. This wasn't just a van. This was *their* van. The same one Mara drove to practice, to the station, to dinner nights. The same one the boys piled into after Little League games. Now, it was a crime scene. Maybe not in the technical sense, but emotionally, spiritually, that's exactly what it was.

I yanked the hose out of the window with more force than I intended. Anger surged through me, at the situation, at the helplessness, at the goddamn sight of that hose. I didn't want the neighbors seeing this. They didn't need this burned into *their* memories too.

"We need to head to the hospital," I said to Jack, my voice remarkably steady, though inside I felt like I was unraveling thread by thread.

I turned to the firefighters, still lingering nearby, their faces painted with the same helplessness I was trying to hide.

"Would you mind standing by until I can get another officer here?" I asked. They nodded immediately. No hesitation. They knew what this was, more than a call. This was one of our own.

As we cleared the cul-de-sac, I saw the Chief's cruiser heading toward us. We stopped, window to window, in the middle of the road. He looked at me, waiting for an update. I was holding it together, barely.

"She was in the van," I told him, trying to keep the emotion out of my voice. "The hose was through the back window. It's Mara."

His face didn't change much, he was always composed, but I could see it hit him behind the eyes.

"Reid's already gone in the ambulance. I don't know her condition yet," I added quickly. "We're heading to the hospital now."

He nodded slowly, then asked, "Did it look suspicious?"

"No," I said. "Not suspicious. But Chief... it's Reid's wife. *It's one of us.* We should call in the State Police."

He shook his head almost instantly. "No. We're keeping it in house."

I stared at him for a moment, disbelief flickering just beneath my restraint. "We need to do this right," I pushed. "I can't, won't, have anyone think we handled this differently because Reid was part of the department."

"I'm not handing this over," he said, firm. "But you don't have to be the one to handle it." Something deep inside me told me that this is the wrong way to handle it, but that wasn't my call.

I took a breath. This was my friend. My shift partner. My firefighter. Our families had dinner together three nights ago.

"If we're doing this in house," I said, locking eyes with him, "then it's going to be me. Jack's already with me"

He paused for a second, then nodded. "Alright. I'll stay and secure the scene."

We pulled away, and I exhaled for what felt like the first time since the call. The weight of the day settled deeper into my chest.

We drove in silence, letting the miles put space between me and the house. My hands gripped the wheel tighter than they needed to, knuckles pale, like I was holding back something bigger than grief. There was no siren, and the radio chattered away but I didn't hear any of it. The storm still building behind my ribs. But even as I pulled farther away, I couldn't outrun the weight pressing in, the sense that something wasn't right. And beneath all of it, a memory rose. One I hadn't thought about in years. The night Sue called. The storm. The roof. The way Reid showed up without hesitation.

Chapter Two

It was one of those brutal New England nights where the cold wasn't just cold, it was bone deep, relentless. The kind of cold that makes you pull your coat tighter, not just because of the wind, but because it settles inside you like a weight.

I was away at the Police Academy when it happened. Sue woke to water coming in the house, the roof was frozen solid, glassy with ice, and as the temperature raised and the rain came, it wasn't gentle. It slammed down hard and fast, relentless, pounding like it had a purpose. Sue was alone with the kids and was unable to reach me, water was pouring into the house. She needed help, she didn't hesitate, she called Reid. Because back then, we all trusted each other without question.

They showed up late that night. No questions asked. In the freezing cold, in the dark, with the rain hammering windows and the roof leaking like a sieve, they did what needed to be done. They didn't wait for thanks or recognition. They just showed up, because that's who they were. Good friends, good men, reliable when it mattered most.

That's the kind of bond we had. At work, we had each other's backs. Off duty, it was no different. We weren't just coworkers; we were something more. A brotherhood forged through long nights, tough calls, shared silences in cruisers, and moments like that, when there's no reason to help except that it's simply what good people do.

Reid had been with me at the PD for a while by then. I'd trained him when he first came on, and over time, he'd become my right hand. Dependable, solid, and calm when it counted. Whether chasing a lead or talking someone down from the edge, we worked together seamlessly, a team without words.

Not long before that night, we'd brought Jack on board. Another local smart, forward thinking, and tough in all the ways that mattered. The kind of guy who could handle himself in a fight but also knew when to listen, when to back off, and when to push. I was training him just like I had with Reid. It already felt like we'd known each other for years.

Work was a balance between pressure and camaraderie. We joked, we pushed each other, and we made the long shifts pass with laughter and sometimes a little friendly rivalry. But when the call came in, the jokes stopped, and the focus snapped into place. We respected the work, and more than that, we respected each other.

We weren't just police officers together. We were firefighters too. The three of us ran calls, trained side by side, and stood shoulder to shoulder in smoke filled hallways and on icy roads. We knew each other's rhythms, strengths, and limits.

We knew each other's families. Our wives were close friends. Our kids played together in backyards and schoolyards. We had dinners and barbecues, game nights that stretched late into the evening, and quiet moments where we just existed as normal people outside the badge.

Reid's full-time job was at the elementary school; he worked as a custodian and bus driver. It was a role he chose deliberately, keeping himself close to his kids every day. That's part of what made him so well known in town, not just as a cop or firefighter, but as a friend and a devoted father. Everyone knew Reid and Mara as the quintessential family: the kind of Hollywood picture perfect setup with two energetic boys, a big beautiful three bedroom, two-bath house on a quiet cul-de-sac. Neighbors often saw them laughing together in the yard, the parents always smiling, sharing the kind of moments that made it clear this was a family who treasured their time together.

Working in my line of work, you'd think I'd always expect the unexpected, and usually, I do. But sometimes, life still manages to surprise you in ways you never imagine.

One time, I was called to check a burglar alarm at what should've been a straightforward scene. The kind of routine you take for granted. But when I got there, the basement door was slightly ajar. That immediately set off alarms in my head. I drew my gun and cautiously made my way down the stairs.

What hit me first was the stench it was thick, rancid, and almost suffocating. I gagged, my stomach twisting as I moved further inside. The basement was packed from floor to ceiling with garbage bags hundreds of them. Rotting food, maggots crawling in the wet leaks pooling on the floor. A nightmare hiding in the shadows.

And yet, when I stepped outside again, everything looked normal. The house was a classic Victorian beauty, pristine and proud. The lawn perfectly manicured, flower beds neat and blooming. A gleaming Mercedes sat parked in the driveway, as if nothing was out of place.

Inside, the upper floors were immaculate, clean furniture, polished floors, family photos smiling down from the walls. It was a picture-perfect home.

It was a jarring contradiction. How could this beautiful household such chaos and decay beneath its foundation? How could the family who lived here let things get that far?

That's the thing about emergency services; you learn quickly that the outside world rarely tells the full story. People carry struggles and pain that don't show up on the surface. Sometimes, those hidden battles are the most dangerous, and the hardest to see.

This moment stuck with me. It's a reminder that what's visible is only part of the story. It's a lot like the work I do every day, sometimes, the real crisis is buried deep, invisible until you're forced to confront it head-on.

I thought I knew Reid and Mara well. I trusted them. They were solid. Dependable. The kind of people you believe when they show you their best selves, not because you're naïve, but because they've earned it. Reid was always calm, always steady. Mara had a laugh that could change the mood of a whole room. Together, they looked like they had it figured out. The kind of couple you'd point to and say, "That's what it's supposed to look like." The kind of family you'd use as your measuring stick.

I did believe in them. I never questioned it. Not once. If you'd asked me a week before that day, I would've told you that they had one of the strongest marriages I knew. That their kids were lucky. That they had something real. I would've staked my reputation on it.

But the truth I was about to uncover had nothing to do with broken trust. It wasn't betrayal, not to me. It was something else entirely. It was quiet pain, isolation, pressure. It was the weight of expectations, of pretending everything was okay when it wasn't. It was two people carrying more than they ever let on, choosing silence over burdening the people around them.

They weren't lying to me. They were surviving in the only way they knew how. Smiles at dinner, shared stories, family photos, the cul-de-sac cookouts. That wasn't fake, it just wasn't the whole picture.

That, in many ways, was even harder to process. Because I did know them. I did love them. Still, I didn't see it. None of us did.

These secrets, they weren't just personal tragedies. They would start to infect everything. Erode the very foundation of what I believed we stood for. Because this wasn't just about Reid and Mara anymore. As the truth started to unspool, it began to undermine every reason I'd wanted to bring in the State Police from the beginning.

We were a small department. Tight knit. Respected, but under a microscope like every other force in the country. The last thing anyone wanted was for us to be investigating one of our own. Once the rumors started and the whispers about bias, coverups, about protecting "our brother" the trust we'd earned over years started to crack.

Accusations came fast. People who had known us their whole lives suddenly wanted to believe the worst. That we were hiding the truth. That we were shielding Reid. That we were covering up a murder.

I can't blame them entirely. From the outside, it must have looked like the classic case, insiders protecting insiders, playing damage control while a family crumbled. But that couldn't have been further from the truth. We weren't circling the wagons; we were struggling to hold on to what little clarity we had. The deeper I got, the more I realized: this wasn't going to be something I could cleanly separate from my own life. It was already too late for that.

What I was uncovering didn't just threaten our credibility. It threatened me. My name. My reputation. The weight of every decision I had made, every call I had answered, was now being held up against the shadows Reid and Mara had hidden for so long.

What haunted me most in those early hours, before the formal investigation even began it wasn't the chaos that would follow. It was the silence before it. The stillness of that night at dinner. The way

Mara had laughed at something Sue said, how Reid had sat back in his chair with that content, tired smile he always wore when things felt "normal." That night didn't feel like a goodbye. But in hindsight, maybe there were things in their eyes I didn't want to see.

It's a strange kind of guilt, realizing you missed the signs. Especially in this line of work, where you're trained to notice what others don't. Subtle body language. A shift in tone. A break in routine. You get good at pattern recognition, reading situations before they explode. But when it comes to the people closest to you? That's where the blind spots live. Right where love and loyalty cloud your instincts.

The weight of that, of not seeing it, settled in fast and hard.

I'd stood in rooms filled with grief before. I'd held the hands of survivors, knocked on doors with news that would change someone's life forever. But nothing had prepared me for this this creeping sense that something irreparable had happened just under my nose. That while I was laughing with them, breaking bread and swapping stories, something vital had already broken. Something that wasn't going to be fixed.

Because some wounds you carry in silence. Some battles don't end with sirens or flashing lights. Some stories aren't told until it's far too late.

That's the truth I'm still learning to live with.

I kept replaying those last few months in my mind like a never-ending loop, searching for anything I might have missed. Every conversation, every glance, every small change in behavior suddenly felt loaded with meaning I hadn't noticed before. Reid's steady voice sometimes held a shadow of something else, something heavier. Mara's laughter, usually so genuine and easy, sometimes faltered, like she was holding something back. At the time, I'd brushed it off. We all did. But now, that casual dismissal felt like a mistake.

It's strange how quickly your perspective can change once the illusion starts to crack. You begin to question the simplest moments. The way Reid would pause before answering a question. The way Mara would sometimes seem distracted at dinner, her smile a little too forced.

These were tiny cracks in a facade so carefully built that none of us dared look too closely.

What haunts me most is that those cracks were there for months, maybe longer. Not just visible to me, but to everyone who cared enough to see. But no one wanted to see. Not really. Because seeing meant acknowledging something none of us were prepared to face.

You learn early in this work that silence can be a weapon and a shield. People guard their pain carefully, especially those who have always been the ones to protect others. Reid and Mara were those people. Steady. Dependable. The rock in the storm. So, when the storm was inside their own home, inside their own hearts, they carried it alone.

We talk a lot about trauma in emergency services, the big calls, the disasters, the moments of life and death. But sometimes the most devastating trauma is quieter, more insidious. It builds up in the spaces between calls, in the moments no one sees. The broken conversations, the hidden tears, the smiles that mask the screams inside.

I remember a night not long before everything started to unravel. We were at the firehouse after a gruelling shift. It was one of those rare nights where the weight of the world seemed just a little lighter. We sat around the table, drinking coffee and swapping stories, trying to find laughter in the wreckage of our day. Reid was there, sitting beside Mara, their hands brushing casually on the table. I watched them, like I often did and for a moment, I thought everything really was okay.

But I noticed something else too, a flicker of exhaustion behind Reid's eyes, a tension in the way he shifted in his chair. Mara's smile didn't quite reach her eyes. They were both holding something back, something neither of them would say aloud.

That moment stayed with me, an echo in the back of my mind when I later stood over that wreckage no one could see.

Because that's the cruel paradox of this job. You're trained to see the signs, to notice when someone is in trouble. But sometimes, the people closest to you are the hardest to read. You want to believe in their strength, their resilience, their ability to hold it all together. So, you look away. Or you tell yourself it's nothing.

I carried that weight with me, more than I realized, until it became a burden too heavy to bear alone. The investigation was more than a professional challenge; it was a personal reckoning. I had to confront the fact that sometimes, even the best people break. Sometimes, the ones you trust most are the ones who hurt the most.

It's not just about betrayal or failure. It's about understanding the complexity of human pain, the ways it hides beneath the surface, the ways it warps the people we love without warning.

There was a time I thought I could separate my personal life from the chaos unfolding around me. That my role as a leader, as a protector of the law, could stay clean and untarnished by the messiness of emotion and loyalty. But I was wrong. That line was always blurred.

Because when your friends are the ones under the microscope, when the family you've trusted your life with is torn apart by silence and secrets, the whole world shifts.

Trust fractures, doubt seeps in. You're left trying to pick up the pieces of something you never thought would break.

I won't pretend it was easy. There were nights I lay awake, staring at the ceiling, wondering where I went wrong. What signs I missed. What I could have done differently. I questioned myself in ways I never had before, my judgment, my instincts, my ability to protect those I cared about most.

But in the end, the truth is rarely clean or simple. It's messy and complicated, like the people we are. Like the lives we lead.

Sometimes, the hardest thing you can do is to face that truth head-on.

Chapter Three

We didn't talk much on the way to the hospital, or at least I don't remember if we did. It was about a 20-minute drive, but it passed like smoke. My thoughts flickered, sharp one moment, completely gone the next. The heater buzzed, and the wipers squeaked across the windshield in a slow rhythm, but none of it registered as sound. Everything inside me had gone silent. Not peaceful, just hollow. I was aware but removed. Present in the physical sense, but emotionally somewhere just outside of it all. Like I was watching a version of myself from a different seat.

The sun was already high, washing the road in a hard, white light that made the world look flat and unreal. It should have been a normal Sunday church bells, lawnmowers in the distance, maybe pancakes and cartoons in a quieter household. But for us, the world had cracked open in the middle of a morning that hadn't even settled into itself yet.

I pulled around back, near the ambulance bay, the entrance that's never lit quite right, even in broad daylight. The shadows stretched long and sharp along the pavement, like the building was trying to pull me in by force. I'd parked there a hundred times before, under far different circumstances. I could picture my old boots hitting this pavement, brisk steps toward the doors, heart racing for someone else's emergency. But today, I wasn't there as part of the system. I wasn't responding to chaos.

I was walking into it from the wrong end, as someone connected to the victim. That made everything feel warped, like I was stepping into a familiar nightmare that had suddenly changed the rules. The balance had shifted, and I was on the wrong side of the equation.

The double doors opened with a hiss, spilling that cold hospital light into the parking lot like a breath held too long. I stepped inside. The ER felt deceptively quiet. Two nurses behind the triage desk looked up from their conversation. One was sipping from a coffee cup, the other flipping through a chart. It could have been a Tuesday night lull. Just another ordinary shift.

But when their eyes landed on me, everything shifted. Their faces dropped casual disappeared in an instant. Recognition set in like a ripple across water, followed quickly by a silence that said more than words ever could. I didn't have to say a word. One of them pointed silently down the hallway to the corner room. I already knew which one she meant.

That room.

I've walked into that room more times than I'd like to admit, though rarely for someone I knew. It's not a patient room in the traditional sense, it's the one they keep for the moments after. For when life doesn't come back. For when someone has to say goodbye. It's the room where words fail and silence takes over. Where the fluorescent lighting feels like an assault, and the air always seems a little colder, a little stiller than anywhere else in the building. Time behaves differently in that space, slower, heavier. Like grief has mass.

I pushed open the door gently. It creaked like they always do. The sound cut through me like a splinter.

There she was.

Mara.

Lying still beneath the white hospital sheet, intubation tube still protruding awkwardly from her mouth, her skin pale and empty of warmth. She was covered up to her collarbone, but I could still see how small she looked. Shrunken. Not physically, but in presence. The life that used to animate her, it was gone. Her eyes were closed, but not gently. They hadn't closed naturally. There was no peace there, no softness. Just stillness. A kind of stillness that makes your bones ache when you look at it too long.

I took a slow step in. The room didn't resist me, but it didn't welcome me either. It was a space built for endings, and it clung to that purpose with every sterile surface and muffled echo.

Reid stood to her left. His posture was slack, arms hanging uselessly at his sides. He didn't move when I entered. Didn't flinch. Just stared at her like he was trying to memorize the shape of her face in case it ever started to fade. He looked shattered, but not in the way I expected. There was a distance to him, a heaviness that didn't look like fresh grief. It looked older, worn, like something that had been living inside him for a while.

"Hey," he said, barely above a whisper. His voice didn't waver, it was flat, like someone too drained to feel anything more.

"I'm so sorry," I replied, the words flat and empty the moment they left my mouth. But what else could I say? There's no version of a sentence that makes this okay. Nothing to stitch together the rupture in the air between us.

I wanted to ask a dozen questions right then. What happened? When did you find her? Had she said anything? Was she sick? Were there signs? But I didn't. Timing matters. There are moments when the job must pause, when humanity must take precedence. I convinced myself this was one of them.

He didn't look at me again, just kept staring at her. Then he said, "I have to get back home to the kids. They don't know yet."

The words hung there, brittle and wrong. I hesitated, I knew it was a mistake to let him walk away without more. But I also understood, those boys had no idea their world had just detonated. And Reid, whatever his state, was still their father. He was the only anchor they had left.

"Yeah," I said quietly. "Of course."

Then he was gone. No long goodbyes, no breakdowns. Just out the door.

At the time, it felt like the right thing to do. Let him have that moment with his sons. Let him grieve in his own way. But looking back now, it was the first real misstep. One I'd come to regret more than I knew. If I could rewind time, I would've stopped him in that hallway. Pressed him for a timeline, for clarity, for anything. But I didn't. Because he was Reid. Because I trusted him, and that trust, well, trust can blind you.

I stayed behind, alone with Mara.

The room felt colder once Reid left. The chill wasn't in the air; it was in the finality. The knowledge that whatever this was, however, it had unfolded, it had ended here. Though not cleanly, not in a way that felt finished.

I stood there longer than I should have, just staring. Thinking about the last time I saw her alive, her laugh. That spark she always had in her eyes; it didn't match the body on the table. None of this made sense.

Eventually, I stepped out, took a long breath. Pushed it all down and walked to the nurse's station.

The charge nurse handed me a clipboard. Her eyes were soft, but her demeanor was clinical; she'd done this before. The paper trail of death, the pronouncement of time, the details of the EMS run, the list of attending staff. I signed it all, asked a few procedural questions.

"Was she conscious when they arrived? Did she say anything? Any injuries?"

The nurse shook her head slowly, her expression already giving away the answer.

"No, unconscious on arrival, vitals were non-existent. They worked her for a while, but…" Her voice softened, "…she..."

I stood still for a second, letting the words settle. Not unexpected, but final.

I asked what she had been wearing. The nurse hesitated for a moment, then replied with a quiet professionalism that nurses seem to carry in these moments.

"She arrived naked."

I blinked, that landed differently.

Naked?

No pyjamas, no robe, nothing?

That didn't track, It didn't make sense for what we'd just seen. I made a mental note, careful not to let it show on my face. Could be nothing. But it felt like something.

I nodded, keeping my voice measured. "Thank you."

She gave a soft nod in return, already turning back toward her station. Another emergency, another name, another case.

I checked the boxes, confirmed the details, signed where I needed to.

Then I stepped back into the hallway, the fluorescent lights buzzing low above me. Everything looked the same as it always did here the polished floors, quiet voices, the smell of antiseptic.

But something was off, I could feel it in my chest before I could name it.

I didn't linger.

I just walked out.

Once outside, I called the Chief.

"She didn't make it," I said.

There was a pause on the other end, heavy.

"Where's Reid?"

"Headed home to the boys, they don't know yet."

"I'll meet you there," he said.

The ride back with Jack felt different now. The emotional haze had burned off, replaced by something else, something sharper.

"We treat this from ten thousand feet," I told him. "No assumptions, we're not friends, we're not locals. Just two investigators dropped into a case we've never seen."

He gave a short nod.

"When someone dies like this, there are two investigations. The one you do on paper. The one that plays out in your head, trying to make it make sense. You can't let the second one get ahead of the first."

Jack was still green, but he understood enough to nod again. He was in the zone now. I saw the switch flip in his eyes. We both knew we were going back into something that didn't feel quite right.

When we turned down the street, the house looked the same as it had earlier. Still. Too still. Like nothing had happened. But the truth hung over it like a shadow. We knew better.

We stepped out of the car. I paused, took a breath.

"This is where the real work starts."

Chief was already there, met us in the driveway. A couple firefighters lingering. He walked over as we entered.

"I've searched the house. No note anywhere," he said.

I nodded. "Let's go through it all again."

The smell hit me immediately. Not death, cleaning products. Someone had tried to tidy up. But it didn't erase the heaviness in the air. That kind of weight can't be mopped up. It lingers in the walls, in the stillness.

Reid was upstairs with the kids, his parents had arrived to help. I'd let him leave without pressing for more, another mistake.

I shook it off and turned to Jack.

"We'll start from the driveway, work backwards."

We stepped outside again. The van was still parked awkwardly, half in, half out of the garage. The lights inside the van were still on, the front of the van was just inside the garage threshold, like it had been moved slightly forward but never parked properly.

"Why like this?" I muttered. "Why not pull in all the way?"

Jack didn't answer, he just began snapping photos.

Inside the van, Mara's clothes were scattered throughout. The massage gun on the floor of the backseat made no sense. It was just *there*, like an afterthought. But nothing in this job is ever "just" anything.

We collected the hose, bagged it as evidence. I didn't take the massage gun, and I probably should have, another mistake on my part.

I stared back at the door to the house from the garage.

"I need to talk to Reid," I said, mostly to myself.

This wasn't over, it wasn't even close.

The garage was stifling. Not hot, but stale. The air hung heavy, full of metallic residue and the faint chemical stink of automotive fluids and whatever carbon monoxide hadn't yet dissipated.

I stepped toward the van again, letting the scene draw me in more deliberately this time. The hose laying on the ground, right where I left it. I found it in the window, which had been cracked just enough to wedge the tubing in. Classic suicide setup, I'd seen it before. Hell, any search engine could tell you how to do it. That's what unsettled to me: it looked too typical, like a checklist.

I squatted down beside the driver's door, scanning the interior from a new angle. This time, I noticed the clothes.

Mara's clothes were strewn around the van haphazardly. A shirt draped half-off the center console, one bra strap caught under the emergency brake. Her jeans bunched near the floorboard like they'd been pulled off in a hurry. One sock twisted in the footwell of the passenger side. I also noted a couple empty wine coolers, they were not dry, so looked fresh.

There was no order here, no intentionality, it felt chaotic. But why? Why was she hurried? Rushed for what reason?

I stood slowly, eyes narrowing as I took it all in again, not just what was there, but what *wasn't*. No purse, no phone, no suicide note. Just clothes like shed skin and the dull hum of a lie settling into the corners of the van.

Jack stepped into the garage behind me, camera still hanging from his neck.

"You good?" he asked.

"Yeah," I said, still staring. "Just… look at this."

He followed my gaze to the tangle of clothing inside the van.

"Huh," he muttered. "That's… not what I expected."

"Exactly," I said.

"She stripped to commit suicide?"

"Maybe," I said. "But why like this? Why not just leave them outside the van? Why throw them around like she changed in a hurry or didn't finish changing at all?"

He stepped closer, angling for a few more shots.

"You think someone else undressed her?"

"I don't know yet," I said. "But this doesn't feel right."

I pointed toward the hose again. "The setup's perfect, too perfect. Hose was through the back, clean seal, engine running. That's textbook. But this?" I gestured at the scattered clothing. "This looks like noise, like confusion. Something else was happening in here before." And the hose was not in the exhaust when we arrived, it was just hanging from the window.

Jack snapped another photo. "You're saying this might not be suicide."

"I'm saying," I replied slowly, "we need to stop assuming it was."

We worked the scene in silence for a few minutes. Jack taking the pictures, me observing. I kept circling the van, noting every strange little anomaly I hadn't registered before. There were smudges on the inside of the rear driver's side window. Not handprints, but close, something brushed against it. The massage gun lay in the backseat floorboard. I picked it up with gloved hands.

"You see this?" I held it up.

Jack nodded. "Yeah. We bagging it?"

"Nah, it's just odd. Why bring this into the van? If you're ending your life, what's the point of a muscle massager?"

He shrugged. "Maybe it was just in here already."

"Maybe," I said. "Or maybe someone brought it in after."

I turned back to the scattered clothes. This time, I looked for signs of a struggle torn fabric, blood, skin cells caught in seams. Nothing obvious, the whole layout whispered disorder. Not the kind that comes from emotional unravelling. The kind that comes from interference.

"You notice anything in the driver's seat?" I asked.

Jack shook his head. "Seats leaned back a lot, not completely laying but more than a driving position. Keys in the ignition, engine was not running when EMS arrived. No sign of forced entry."

"She was found in the driver's seat?"

"No EMS said she was on the ground with Reid doing CPR." Jack explained.

"Unconscious?"

"Unconscious, not breathing, naked."

I paced toward the rear of the van and looked at the carbon soot lightly dusting the tailgate. I opened it slowly, peered inside. Cargo space was empty except for a towel and a few broken crayons rolling along the floorboard. Family car. The kind that sees ball games and spilled juice and backpacks dropped after school.

It didn't feel like a death scene.

It felt like a cover.

Inside, the house was quiet. Someone had turned off the television. The unnatural calm settled over everything like a fog. Upstairs, I could hear faint murmurs, Reid's voice, maybe, pacing in a room I couldn't see.

I moved through the kitchen next. The trash bin was half-full. Rummaging through it revealed nothing, mostly paper towels, a microwave meal box, and a pair of used latex gloves that made my stomach twist.

I bagged them without a word.

Then I found her phone.

It was on the charger in the hallway. Face down. I called for Jack, and we bagged that too.

I returned to the garage one last time, standing just outside the open door, letting the quiet settle in again. The van sat there like an unanswered question.

The air still hadn't cleared.

Neither had the truth.

Chapter Four

Just as Jack and I were finishing up in the garage, the door to the kitchen creaked open.

Reid stepped down first, followed by the boys and his parents. The boys looked shell-shocked, staring at the floor, pale and quiet in the way kids get when something's knocked the wind out of their world. Their shoulders were drawn up, posture small, as if they were trying to disappear into their own skin. One of them clutched a rumpled corner of his hoodie, fingers twisting the fabric rhythmically, like it was the only thing anchoring him.

His parents flanked them like bookends, solid, quiet, faces carved into solemn lines. No one cried, not in that moment. But the absence of sound was a grief all its own. His mother had a hand on Miles's shoulder, her thumb rubbing slow circles like she could erase the memory from his skin. His father stood still, eyes hard, jaw set like granite. Years of silent strength wrapped around everything he did.

I knelt down, eye-level with the boys. I greeted each of them by name, gently, like I was trying not to shatter what was left of them. One at a time, I gave them a hug, just long enough to be real, not long enough to make it worse.

"I'm here if you need anything, okay?" I told them. "Anything."

They nodded, but didn't speak. Just wide eyes and blank expressions. The way trauma moves into a child's body and sets up camp, quiet but immovable.

Reid caught my eye above their heads.

"I know we need to talk," he said, voice low but steady. "The boys are going to my parents', okay?"

I nodded.

"That's fine."

It was the right call, his folks lived close. The boys didn't need to be here for what came next, whatever form it was going to take. This would give Reid space to speak freely, if that's what he actually planned to do.

They left with a few hushed goodbyes. The car door clicked shut behind them, and just like that, the atmosphere changed. It felt like air being pulled out of a garage.

Now it was just the three of us, Reid, Jack, and me. A familiar triangle. We'd stood together in garages, kitchens, and backyards before. We'd debriefed tragedies, unravelled timelines, processed chaos. We'd done it over beer, over coffee, over long silences. But this time, the air was heavier. Like grief had a body and was sitting in the fourth chair.

We moved back into the kitchen, sat at the table. The same one I'd eaten birthday cake at years ago, the same one where kids had scattered Legos and homework. Now, it felt like an interrogation desk in slow motion.

I leaned in slightly. No notepad, no recorder, just memory and instinct.

"You worked last night, right? Left around midnight?"

Reid nodded. "Yeah."

"And when you got home… what was going on?"

He hesitated, not long, but long enough to register. His eyes flinched. Not closed, but searching, like someone queuing up the right version of events in their head.

"Mara was up waiting for me," he said. "She'd had a couple wine coolers, was a little buzzed. I was surprised to see her still awake."

His eyes flicked briefly toward the garage door. A reflex? Or a tell?

"But as soon as I walked in, I got this gut feeling. Like something was off. Like the front door at the PD didn't latch shut behind me."

He looked at me more directly now, intentional.

"You remember we were having issues with that door?" he asked.

I nodded slowly. "Yeah, I know."

It was true, But the way he said it, it felt planted. Like a subtle misdirection embedded into his alibi.

"And Mara?" I asked. "How'd she react to that?"

He dropped his gaze, fiddled with a thumbnail.

"She got upset, accused me of going to see someone else. She was… insistent."

"Did she mention a name?"

He shook his head. "No, just said I was lying, wouldn't let it go."

I watched his face carefully; the emotional landscape wasn't right. Not sharp enough; not frayed enough for a man whose wife had accused him of cheating hours before she died. Either he'd numbed it all or he was hiding behind a veil of practiced detachment.

"Is there another woman?" I asked, plainly.

He gave a soft, incredulous laugh. Too soft, too smooth. The kind you rehearse to sound dismissive.

"No, come on, you know me."

That line always makes me pause. People say it like its evidence. But sometimes it's a plea.

"I told her it wasn't true," he said. "That I just needed to check the damn door, and I left."

"For how long?"

"Fifteen, twenty minutes max. Door was shut when I got there. Everything locked up, I came straight back."

"And when you walked in?"

"She was still in the kitchen. Had another drink or two. Still upset, but not yelling anymore."

His voice had evened out, but his eyes never quite landed anywhere. They hovered, on the table, on his hands, on the clock behind me. Never on me.

"Then what?" I asked.

"She said she wanted to go out to the van and fool around. Like the old days."

His tone was strange, flat, as if the memory had already turned grayscale in his mind.

"The van was in the garage?" I clarified.

"Yeah. I moved it after I found her," he added.

I held up a hand. "Let's stay in order."

He nodded, reset.

"So, you went out to the van together."

"Yeah."

"Had sex?"

He nodded once. "Yes."

"You both undressed in the van?"

"Yes."

Each answer clipped, mechanical. Too perfect in sequence; like a drill he'd been through already.

"And afterward?"

"We laid there a few minutes, I thought about staying. But I wanted to check on the boys."

"She say anything?"

"No. But… she didn't want me to go. I could tell."

I leaned in. "Did she ask you not to leave?"

He shook his head. "No. Just looked at me, quiet."

There was a pause. One of those uncomfortable ones that opens up space you don't want to be in.

"Then?"

"I threw on my sweatpants and a T-shirt, went upstairs."

"Checked on the boys?"

"Yeah, Miles was half-awake, I laid down with him. He gets restless sometimes."

He stopped, swallowed hard, and sighed.

"What about the massage gun?" I asked.

He looked up at me for the first time, caught off guard.

"She uses that to finish," he said, sheepishly. "That's what she was doing when I went to check on the boys."

"Okay. Then what?"

"I must've dozed off. Next thing I knew, it was morning. Light was coming through the blinds. I was surprised she didn't wake me, she usually does."

He rubbed the bridge of his nose. Tired, but not teary.

"So, I got up, went to our bedroom…"

"She wasn't there," he said. "I checked the bathroom, then went downstairs."

"And?"

"I didn't see her, but I heard the van running in the garage."

The room tightened, that sentence pulls gravity into the floor. My gut wrenched.

"What did you think?" I asked.

"I thought… maybe she fell asleep out there, I said, 'Oh no,' and ran to the garage."

His voice cracked at the edge. The first raw emotion I'd seen, his eyes closed briefly, like he was trying to unsee it.

"It was filled with exhaust. I hit the opener, jumped in. She was on the middle seat. Unconscious. Same place I left her…"

His voice thinned out, barely hanging on.

Jack shifted beside me, finally breaking his stillness.

"You didn't smell the fumes earlier?" he asked gently.

Reid opened his mouth, then closed it. His face twitched, confused, offended, even.

"No… I mean, I was upstairs… I guess I didn't notice…"

I didn't press. Not yet, but I noted it. Filed it alongside everything else.

Something in my gut buzzed, quiet but insistent. Like a thread I hadn't pulled tight yet.

Because nothing about this felt finished, and everything about it felt off.

The phrase stuck. It scratched at something in the back of my skull, refusing to lie still.

"I backed the van out," he continued. "Dragged her onto the driveway. Started CPR. Ran inside, called 911. Then went back out and kept going."

The room was still, Jack's pen had stopped moving.

Reid stared at his hands. Rubbed them slowly. They were clean. Too clean. No sweat, no panic. Just a man with a tidy story and hands that didn't seem to know what panic felt like.

I leaned back, kept it casual.

"Was the van running when you went to check on the boys?"

He blinked. "No."

"She was curled on middle back seat?"

"Yeah. Just like she was when I left."

Again. Just like I left her.

Something in those words refused to sit still.

"I didn't see the hose until after EMS took over," he added, like it was an afterthought.

Then he looked up. His voice changed. Just slightly.

"That's how her father died," he said. "You know that, right?"

Chapter Five

The house was quieter now, too quiet.

Reid had gone upstairs to lie down for a bit. Said he needed a minute, I didn't argue. Grief had its own rhythm, and right now, his was a metronome of exhaustion and shock.

Jack had left not long after the formal interview. He offered a few parting words, supportive, soft, but I could tell the questions lingered with him also. His notepad was full, but it was his silence at the door that said the most.

I stayed behind.

Not just because Reid was my friend, or because the boys might need someone when they came back. I stayed because something didn't sit right. If there was anything I'd learned in 15 years of picking through broken scenes and unravelling stories from the quiet corners, they never sat right by accident.

I stood in the doorway of the garage again, alone this time. The air had cleared, but the weight hadn't. The van sat like a monument, still, quiet. Too quiet. It wasn't evidence, not officially. Not yet, but it was a container of questions, every surface felt like it was whispering.

I walked around the perimeter again, letting my eyes catch on details I'd missed before. A child's sock in the corner, a used tissue tucked under the passenger seat. No signs of a struggle, nothing out of place, and yet, everything was.

Back inside, I poured myself a glass of water and leaned on the counter. The hum of the fridge was the only sound, a low and steady reminder that life was still moving, even if this house had stopped.

Reid's footsteps came slowly down the stairs.

"Thanks for staying," he said.

I nodded. "Of course."

He looked worse than earlier, eyes sunken, voice thin. But there was something else now.

"What now?" he asked

The question hung there, not rhetorical, not defeated. Just hollow, like he was already wading through the motions.

He'd already chosen a funeral home. Said they had a meeting scheduled the next morning to go over arrangements. I offered to go with him, but he shook his head. "Thanks," he said. "But I think I need to do this part myself."

We talked about the boys next. He looked worried, more than I'd seen all day.

"I don't know what to do about suits," he admitted. "They've never had one."

I gave him the name of a place just over the state line, a small shop, quiet and discreet, run by a man who knew how to size a kid without turning it into a trauma. Reid nodded, grateful.

I stayed until his parents returned with the boys. They'd stopped for fast food on the way back, trying to reclaim some sliver of normal. The boys looked a little better, cleaner, fed, but the thousand-yard stare was still there. When they hugged their dad, he held them tighter than I've ever seen him hold anything.

The next morning, I started making calls.

I reached out to the first responders who were on scene. I told myself it was procedural, just due diligence. But I already knew the drill. I wasn't expecting anything different.

At first, I didn't get anything different.

Every one of them said the same thing: they arrived to find Reid performing CPR on Mara in the driveway. She was completely naked. The van had already been backed out. The garage doors were wide open, and the smell of exhaust still clung to the air. No one mentioned seeing anything that raised flags. All agreed the hose was not in the exhaust.

Except one.

A young firefighter I'd known for a while. He called me back late in the afternoon, almost like he wasn't sure if he should say anything.

"There's one thing I didn't put in the report," he said. "Didn't know if it mattered."

"Tell me anyway," I said.

"It's the boys," he said. "They were upstairs. Watching."

"Watching what?"

He exhaled. "The whole thing, from the bedroom window. They saw everything."

Everything?.

Their mother, naked. Their father trying to bring her back. The flashing lights, the shouting, the chaos. All of it, framed like a silent film in the pane of that upstairs window.

"They never came outside," he added. "Just stood there, faces pressed to the glass."

I closed my eyes for a second. That image would stay with me.

"No one checked them," he said. "For CO poisoning, I mean."

He was right. In the scramble, no one had thought to assess the kids. It was a lapse, no question, but one I understood. Everyone on that scene had known Reid and Mara. They'd responded with their hearts first. Sometimes that gets in the way of the protocol.

But now that crack in the process was part of the story, too. Just like the things Reid wasn't saying. Just like the way her body was found.

Just like the words he'd said, twice now, without even realizing it:

"Same place I left her"

Just after that, I got a call from the State Medical Director.

He didn't waste time with pleasantries.

"She had a significant blood alcohol level," he said. "But I have one question for you. The hose, did it have soot or exhaust residue on the end that was in the tailpipe?"

I paused. I hadn't really thought to look at it that closely in the moment.

"When the first responders arrived," I said, "the hose was *out* of the exhaust. Not attached."

"Was that how you found it?" he asked.

I hesitated. "Yes."

Silence. Then: "Anything about the scene strike you as suspicious?"

I wanted to say yes. I wanted to unload every nagging detail that hadn't sat right since the garage. But suspicion without proof is just noise.

"All I really have is history," I finally said. "Her father died by suicide. Same method, and Mara saw it."

The doctor was quiet for a moment. Then he said, almost to himself, "It's not unheard of, someone mimicking a parent's suicide. Especially when they witnessed it."

A pause.

"You still have the hose?"

"Yes."

"Do me a favor? Go rub the end of it. See if there's residue, anything that suggests it was in contact with a tailpipe."

I placed him on hold and went straight to the evidence locker.

The hose was coiled in a sealed bag, the kind we used for storing bulkier evidence. I opened it and pulled the hose out carefully. It was just a standard wet/dry vacuum hose, the kind you could find at any hardware store. Lightweight. Plastic. Ridged.

I rubbed my hand along one end, then the other.

Black smudges.

Both sides.

I stared at my palm. Yes, there was something there, but not much. A faint smear, like charcoal dust. It could be exhaust residue. Or it could just be dirt. This hose wasn't new, it had been used before, maybe stored in a garage, rolled around in the back of a van. There were a dozen ways it could've picked up grime.

Still, I picked up the phone the Medical Director was still waiting.

"Both ends had black on them," I said. "Not a lot. But it left marks."

He exhaled, satisfied. "Okay. That helps." He answered satisfied.

But it didn't feel settled for me.

That hose is the single detail I've second-guessed more than any other. Not the returning for the door. Not the giving him more time before questioning, or the polished timeline. That hose.

Because yes, there was black on it.

But what was it?

Soot? Dirt? Something left over from a project?

Or was I just seeing what I needed to see?

At the end of the day, I headed back over to Reid's, not as an investigator, not with questions. Just as a friend.

We didn't talk much at first. We sat in the quiet hum of his living room, the kind of silence that doesn't need to be filled. Eventually, he started talking. No prompting, no agenda. Just… words spilling out because they had to go somewhere.

He told me about the funeral home visit that morning. How the hardest part, worse than the garage, worse than the hospital, was walking into that room full of caskets.

"She was always so full of life," he said, voice cracking. "There I was… picking a box to put her in."

He looked away, jaw clenched.

"I broke down right there. Couldn't breathe. I didn't think I'd make it through the door, let alone through that."

There wasn't anything to say that would make it better. So, I didn't try. I just sat there and let him carry the weight out loud for a while. He needed that more than anything else.

The next morning, Jack rode with me. Neither of us said much at first, coffee in hand, the road rolling out in front of us. It was the kind of quiet that comes after a heavy week, the kind that gives space for things to surface.

After a few miles, he finally spoke.

"I didn't want to bring this up last night," he said, eyes forward. "But I've been hearing things."

I glanced over. "What kind of things?"

He hesitated.

"Rumors," he said. "About Reid. About him… maybe seeing someone."

My gut tightened.

"Do you know who?"

He shook his head. "Don't have a name. Just that she lives out past Route 12, near the old marina. Friend of a friend kind of thing. Might be nothing, but it's out there."

I nodded, filed it away. We'd follow up.

We stopped at a gas station just off the highway, one of those old corner stores with sticky floors and sun-faded ads in the window. I pumped while Jack went in to grab snacks.

That's when a man approached me. Mid-forties maybe, ballcap low, face tight with something coiled just under the surface.

"You're working that thing with the cop's wife, right?" he asked, low and direct.

I turned slowly. "That's right."

He glanced toward the store, then back at me. "You really oughta take a closer look at Reid."

"What makes you say that?"

He snorted. "Because I think he's been screwin' around with my wife. I'm not the only one who knows it."

The air shifted. My instincts kicked in.

"You have a name?" I asked.

He didn't answer right away. Ya Crystal, but we are separated now. After this happened, I told her to leave, and not to have my kids around that murderer!"

I cautioned him on outright accusations. "Can you give me a statement with facts of this?"

"No," he finally muttered. "Not right now. Just… check your facts. All I'm saying is things ain't adding up."

He walked off before I could push further. By the time Jack came out, the guy was gone.

"Who was that?" Jack asked.

"Not sure yet," I said. "But the air around this thing just got a little thicker."

As we drove, I told Jack what the man at the gas station had said. Jack shifted in his seat, uncomfortable.

"I've been wondering the same," he admitted. "I've seen Reid's truck over at her place a couple of times, late."

I shot him a look. "You're just now saying this?"

He raised his hands. "I wasn't sure, I didn't want to throw around speculation, especially not now. I didn't know if it meant anything."

I didn't respond right away. Just stared ahead at the road as the weight of it settled in. The man's accusation, Jack's confirmation, and now a name, Crystal.

It was time to talk to Reid again.

We pulled up to the house. He stepped outside as soon as he saw us, concern already on his face. I waved him over and led him toward the cruiser, away from the house and any ears.

I got straight to it.

"Reid, I need to ask you something directly. What's going on with you and Crystal?"

He froze. Took a long breath and dropped his eyes to the gravel.

"Yeah… kinda," he said.

"Kinda?" I repeated. "What does that mean?"

He started down the usual path. "We're just friends, hanging out,"

"Bullshit," I cut in, firm. "Be straight with me. You know I'll find out one way or another."

He winced, then nodded slowly.

"Okay. Sorry. It's tough, man," he said. "Mara and I… we've been having problems for a while. We weren't intimate anymore. Not even close. Me and Crystal… we just got comfortable. It wasn't planned. She's been separating from her husband too. I knew it was just a matter of time before Mara and I split."

Did Mara agree there were issues? Did she know you were contemplating separation? Have you talked to a lawyer about divorce?

His words hung there in the air, heavy and flat.

I let it settle before saying anything else. There it was the first honest crack in the foundation. Not just tension, but motive. Something real.

"Does anyone else know?" I asked.

He shook his head. "Not really. I mean… probably people guessed. But no one knew for sure."

Jack and I exchanged a glance.

The pieces were starting to shift, and not in Reid's favor.

So, Reid was cheating on Mara, with a married woman named Crystal. That much was out in the open now. The admission was raw, reluctant, and loaded with justification. But infidelity, no matter how tangled or emotional, didn't automatically equal murder. People cheat every day. People get separated, fall out of love, slip into the arms of someone new. It's messy, sometimes cruel, but it's not always criminal.

Still, in the context of everything else, the timing, the staged feel of the garage, the boys watching from upstairs, the subtle inconsistencies in his story, it couldn't be ignored. Affairs create motive, motive changes everything.

We were no longer just looking at a tragic death. We were standing at the edge of something darker, something layered. This wasn't about grief anymore, it was about secrets. About who knew what, and when.

Crystal had just become central.

We needed to talk to her. Not just to confirm the relationship, but to get a sense of what she knew about Reid's marriage, about Mara, about that morning. Because if she was part of this before Mara died, if there were texts, calls, visits, arguments, then she might hold the key to what really happened in that garage.

And maybe… just maybe… she already suspected more than she'd let on.

Chapter Six

Crystal sat stiffly across from me in the small, windowless conference room, her hands folded tightly in her lap, knuckles pale beneath the soft knit of her cardigan. Her eyes flicked from corner to corner, not looking at me, not looking at anything directly, like she was hoping to find an escape route etched somewhere in the paint. The hum of the overhead fluorescent lights buzzed in the silence between us, a low, sterile soundtrack to her unravelling.

She was younger than I expected, thirties maybe, but there was something prematurely tired in her eyes. Not age exactly, more like erosion. Life had worn through her outer layer, exposing something raw underneath. For a town this size, I should've recognized her. But I didn't. That anonymity in a place where everyone knows everyone? That was its own kind of red flag.

When I asked about her relationship with Reid, she didn't flinch. But her words came clipped and overly calm, like she'd memorized them in the mirror.

"We worked together at the school. That's it."

Her voice was steady, but her hands betrayed her, fingers clenched, thumb rubbing furiously at a spot on her palm like she was trying to erase a memory written on her skin.

I leaned forward, lowering my voice but not softening it. "We know what's going on."

She blinked.

"You're not helping yourself by lying," I continued. "Obstruction's a real charge, Crystal. You're already separated, right? Who are you protecting? Reid?"

I gave it a beat before the final push.

"Mara is dead, we've already spoken to Reid."

Crystal's jaw trembled slightly before she locked it again. A tear broke free from one eye and slid down her cheek. She wiped it away quickly, the motion sharp with shame. Then she dropped her gaze, staring at her hands like they might hold the answers instead of the evidence.

Her breath came out in a slow, shaky sigh, like she'd been holding it for far too long.

"It wasn't supposed to be anything serious," she said, her voice barely above a whisper. "At least not at first."

Gone was the polished tone. Gone was the script. This was the real Crystal emerging, guard down, edges fraying.

"We started talking more after one of the school safety meetings," she continued. "He stayed behind to help clean up. So, did I. We talked about protocols, drills, how dumb the district's policies were. That kind of thing."

She sniffed, cleared her throat.

"It was harmless at first. Lunchroom conversations. Little texts about work. Jokes about teachers we didn't like. Then it got… personal. He told me about the problems he and Mara were having. Said they barely spoke at home. That it had been like that for years."

She looked up at me then, and I saw it, shame tangled with a sort of desperate sincerity.

"I believed him. I mean, I *wanted* to believe him. We were both stuck, both unhappy. It felt easy, natural. Like I could finally breathe with someone again."

I let the silence stretch long and deliberate. People will often keep talking just to fill it. Crystal was no exception.

"I didn't mean to hurt anyone," she said. "I sure as hell didn't think it would end like this."

"Did Mara know?" I asked.

She hesitated, lips parting, then nodded slowly.

"I think so. I mean, I never told her. But... yeah. I felt it. She looked at me different the last time I saw her, like she'd figured me out. No words. Just a look."

"When was that?"

"About a week before she died. We had that spring showcase at the school, the one with the student art displays. She was there with the boys. She didn't say much. Just walked by me like I didn't exist."

She twisted a tissue in her hands now, tearing it at the edges.

"I told Reid I thought she knew. He said not to worry."

I studied her face, watching for micro-reactions, little betrayals of truth or deceit. She didn't flinch. The emotion was real. But that didn't mean the full story was.

"Did Reid ever talk about leaving Mara? Custody, the house, finances?"

Crystal's throat moved in a tight swallow.

"He said they'd talked about separating, after the school year. He didn't want to disrupt the kids' routine. Said Mara wasn't doing well. Mentally. He was scared a breakup would push her over the edge."

"Did he ever say he thought she'd hurt herself?"

She shook her head emphatically.

"No, he said she could be... volatile, moody. But he never said anything about suicide. If I'd known," Her voice cracked, and she buried her face in her hands. "God, if I'd known she was in that place..."

I waited, letting her cry, giving her the dignity of silence. Then I handed her another tissue.

"Crystal," I said carefully, "do you think Reid could've hurt her?"

Her eyes snapped up to meet mine. Wide, wet, defiant.

"No," she said. "No, I mean, he's not *like that*. He's not violent. He gets frustrated, sure. But he loves those boys, he'd never do something that would take him away from them."

"But Mara was in the way, wasn't she?"

Her jaw tightened. "No. She was… she was broken. I don't think Reid hated her. I think he pitied her, he felt trapped."

"Did the two of you ever talk about life without her in it?"

Crystal opened her mouth, then stopped. Her eyes darted to the corner of the table.

That half-second pause told me everything.

"We might've joked," she said finally. "Not about killing her. Just… 'what ifs.' What if we were free, what if we didn't have to sneak around. But it was never serious."

I leaned back, letting the weight of her words settle between us. A week ago, Crystal was just background noise. Now, she was center frame.

"What about your husband?" I asked. "Did he know?"

She winced. "He knew I was spending time with Reid. He didn't love it, but he thought it was just friendship."

"And now?"

"He kicked me out after Mara died. Said he didn't want to be part of any of it. I'm staying in our rental house."

"Why now?" I asked.

"Because he's not blind, I wasn't hiding it very well toward the end."

"Did you and Reid text on your regular phones? Or did either of you have burner phones or multiple phones?"

"I only have one, but I know he has two, he says one is strictly work"

"All right," I said finally. "That's all for now. But stay available, we may need to talk again."

She nodded, eyes down, gathering her things slowly, carefully, as if buying time before walking back out into a world that suddenly saw her differently.

I watched her leave. Her posture was still rigid, but lighter now, like confession had pulled a weight off her shoulders. Unfortunately, it landed on mine instead.

Jack stepped into the room as she disappeared down the hall, arms folded across his chest.

"She crack?"

"She didn't break," I said. "But she definitely bent."

He raised an eyebrow. "So where does that leave us?"

I stared at the door a moment longer before answering.

"It means Mara knew, and this wasn't just a marriage falling apart, it was a pressure cooker. Something was going to blow."

Jack gave a slow nod, already reaching for his phone.

"We need to talk to Mara's therapist," I said. "If she had one, I want to know where her head really was, not just what Reid says."

"On it," he said, stepping out to make the call.

I turned back to the table. Crystal's tissue sat there like evidence, damp, crumpled, intimate. A small, human artifact in the middle of something rapidly turning clinical.

The story was changing shape again, I had the feeling it was far from finished.

I decided it was time. We weren't going to get the rest of the story through polite conversation and sideways glances. The narrative was shifting, too many pauses, too many "what ifs," and just enough contradiction to demand a deeper dive. I drafted two warrants: one for Crystal's phone and computer, and one for Reid's.

We agreed to go after Reid's first. If he got wind Crystal had been pulled in or that she'd talked more than she intended, it could all unravel. We needed to hit this clean and fast, before he had time to scrub anything, or worse, vanish into a story we couldn't verify.

We pulled into his driveway just after five. His truck wasn't there, and no one came to the door when we knocked. The house was quiet, too quiet, like it was holding its breath.

Just as we turned back toward the cruiser, headlights rounded the corner. Reid's truck. The boys were in the backseat, their faces pressed against the glass with the kind of casual boredom only kids can muster on a weekday evening when their world has already tilted off its axis.

Reid parked and stepped out, offering a polite but tired smile.

"Evening," I greeted, watching the boys scramble out and head up the walk.

"Hey," he replied, voice low. He turned to the boys, "Go on in, I'll be there in a sec."

They disappeared inside, the door closing behind them with a hollow thunk. Then it was just the two of us in the driveway, tension bleeding into the quiet around us.

"What's up?" he asked.

"How you holding up?" I asked, not as small talk, but because I honestly didn't know anymore.

He sighed, rubbing a hand down his jaw. "I'm hoping better after the funeral tomorrow. Maybe get some kind of closure. It's all just... a blur right now."

"I get it," I said. "I know it's confusing. Unfair, and a mess on top of it. Are you all set? Anything I can do to help?"

"I think we're good. Just trying to keep the boys busy. They don't get it yet, how could they? I barely do."

I nodded slowly. "Well, I'll be at the wake tonight if you need anything. But there's one thing we have to take care of today."

His eyes narrowed a little, not suspicion, yet, but the look of a man bracing for another emotional gut punch.

"I told you I'm here to help," he said. "What is it?"

"I need your electronics, your computer, any laptops or tablets, and your phone."

There was a pause. A beat too long.

"Now?" he asked, voice pitching slightly. "I mean… today? I need my phone, man. Everything's on there."

"I know," I said calmly. "But we need to preserve any communication between you and Crystal, and anyone else connected to the case. I brought you a burner phone, basic, but it'll get you through the next few days."

I reached into the passenger seat and pulled out the shrink-wrapped phone from the evidence bag, still in the box.

He stared at it like it was a snake.

"You serious?" he said finally, eyes flicking to the house, then back to me. "I've got pictures of the boys on there. Messages from people who are just trying to support me through this. I'm not hiding anything."

"If that's true, this will help confirm it," I said evenly. "You said yourself, you want answers, so do I. This is part of that process."

He exhaled slowly, and I could see the fight happening behind his eyes. There was a part of him that wanted to blow up, to lash out and say no. But something stopped him. Maybe guilt. Maybe the weight of being the grieving husband in a small town where people were already starting to whisper.

"Fine," he said, pulling the phone from his pocket. "But I want it back."

"You'll get it back. Once the tech team's done pulling the data. Shouldn't take more than a few days."

He turned toward the house. "I'll grab the laptop."

I watched him go, uneasy. He wasn't yelling. He wasn't resisting. But he wasn't relieved either. His cooperation felt… strategic, measured.

When he returned, he handed over a slim MacBook in a padded sleeve. "That's it," he said. "No tablet. Just this and the phone."

I took the items and started logging them into evidence bags.

"One more thing, Reid," I added, looking up. "Do you have a second phone? For work maybe?"

His expression changed, subtle, but enough. His eyes didn't quite meet mine when he answered.

"No. Just the one."

I nodded slowly, letting the silence thicken for a second. "That's strange. Crystal mentioned you had a second line. Said it was something you used for school stuff or work messages you didn't want on your personal phone."

His mouth opened, then closed. A quick recalibration behind the eyes. "That was months ago," he finally said. "Old phone. School gave it to me for one of the programs. I turned it back in when the grant ended. Didn't think it mattered."

"It might," I said. "Did you erase it before turning it in?"

"I think so. I don't know, I factory reset it or something. Why?"

I let the question hang. "Just need to know where it is now. Who has access. If it's sitting in a drawer at the school, I need to pull it too."

He gave a stiff nod, jaw clenched. "I'll call the school tomorrow, see if they still have it. Probably junked it."

"Appreciate it," I said.

He looked like he wanted to say more but didn't. Just nodded again and went back into the house, the door clicking shut with finality.

Jack leaned against the cruiser, arms folded. "That could've gone worse."

"Yeah," I said. "But it also could've gone a hell of a lot better."

We drove off in silence, the sky dimming behind us. As we headed toward the lab, my phone buzzed. Text from forensics: *Pulling*

Crystal's phone now. Already a few interesting messages flagged. I will keep you posted.

Whatever Reid thought he'd buried, whatever Crystal thought she could contain, it was time to dig it all up.

Because someone wasn't telling the whole truth.

Now, we had the keys to find it.

But we still had a problem.

The second phone.

Whether Reid was downplaying it or outright lying, I didn't know yet. But I wasn't going to wait around for him to get his story straight or start making calls to clean things up. Crystal had been clear: the second phone existed. I had a feeling it wasn't just for "school business." People don't hide harmless things.

Fortunately, we had a lead. The school principal, Stephen Madsen, lived just a few streets over. He was a straight shooter, one of those guys who ran parent-teacher conferences like incident command briefings. He was also a captain on the fire department, which meant I'd worked with him on more than one late-night structure fire and knew his tell when something rattled him.

We pulled up to his house just after six. American flag out front. Pickup in the drive. Lights on in the kitchen. Small-town predictability I was suddenly grateful for.

I turned to Jack. "We need to get ahead of this before Reid makes a call."

Jack nodded. "You think he will?"

"If he hasn't already, he's thinking about it."

We walked up the driveway and knocked. Stephen answered the door in a pair of sweatpants and a faded department hoodie, a kid's cartoon playing low in the background. He looked surprised to see us, concern flickering across his face.

"Evening, Capt.," I greeted.

"Hey," he said, stepping outside and pulling the door halfway closed behind him. "Everything all right?"

"Yeah," I said. "Just need a minute. Not a big deal, but something came up related to the school's tech equipment. Mind if we ask about a phone that might've been issued to Reid?"

Stephen furrowed his brow. "A phone? Like a district phone?"

"Reid mentioned he had a second phone through the school. Said it was related to one of the safety or grant programs."

"Oh… yeah." He nodded slowly, piecing it together. "That would've been last fall. We had a pilot program that funded a few staff phones for internal messaging, district only lines, encrypted messaging between admin and safety leads. Didn't last long. The funding ran out early."

"Did Reid return the phone?"

Stephen scratched the back of his head. "They were supposed to be turned back in when the pilot ended. I know I got most of them… honestly, I'd have to check inventory. I don't remember if his specifically came back."

"Where would it be if it wasn't returned?" I asked.

"If it's still out there, it's either buried in his desk at school… or he kept it."

"Could you check your records tonight?" I asked. "We're trying to account for all devices that could hold relevant data. If the phone's still in circulation, we'll need to secure it."

He hesitated, not in defiance, but in calculation. He knew enough from his fire department side to read the subtext.

"This about Mara?"

I didn't answer directly. "Just trying to button everything up. Dot i's, cross t's. If it turns out nothing's on it, great. But we need to be thorough."

He nodded again, this time with more gravity. "All right. I'll check the device log and any old records from the pilot. If the phone's still out there, I'll help you track it down."

"Also, what do you know about Reid and Crystals relationship?

"Um, I see them hanging at school and I know they are friends. I have heard the rumors but I never have seen anything like that, and I hate rumors"

"Ya I get that, how long ago did you hear these rumors?"

"I don't know for sure, somewhere along the way this past school year"

"Appreciate it, and Stephen, keep this between us for now. We don't want to set off any alarms before we know what we're dealing with."

"You got it."

As we stepped back toward the cruiser, I felt that shift again, the kind you don't see until you're halfway through a case and suddenly, the pieces start sliding into place in a way that makes your stomach tighten. This wasn't about a forgotten school-issued device anymore.

This was about what was on it.

Jack glanced over as we got in. "Think he'll find it?"

"Ya I do I think it was turned in" I said. "Hopefully for Reid."

Jack didn't say anything. Just started the engine.

Time to get back to the station. We have to change for the wake.

Chapter Seven

The parking lot was already full when I arrived at the funeral home. Neatly dressed couples walked in pairs, heads low, some carrying flowers, others just holding tightly to each other. A few firefighters I recognized stood out front, their dress blues pressed and uncomfortable, fidgeting like they didn't know where to put their hands.

I wasn't here in an official capacity tonight. Holding my wife's hand as we entered. Not technically. This was about supporting a friend, showing my face, being part of the grieving community. But the lines between personal and professional had blurred so far, I wasn't sure they existed anymore.

Inside, the air was thick with too much cologne and muffled sorrow. Soft organ music floated from the speakers, and Mara's photo slideshow flickered against one wall, a loop of bright smiles and beach trips, PTA meetings, and holiday mornings. I stood in the back for a long minute, just watching the images roll past.

It didn't match what I'd seen on that table.

Reid spotted me from across the room and gave a small nod. He looked older, like the past few days had aged him ten years. His tie was crooked. His boys clung to either side of him like life preservers.

"Thanks for coming," he said when I stepped up.

"Wouldn't be anywhere else," I said. "You holding up?"

"Trying, It's a lot."

I nodded. "If you need to step out at any point, just say the word."

He gave me a weak smile, grateful but distant. I didn't press him; this wasn't the moment.

The line moved slowly past the casket. Mara lay surrounded by white lilies, her face softened by makeup and gentle lighting.

I stepped aside to let the next mourner forward and wandered toward the edge of the room. I didn't wear a uniform, but people still recognized me. A few offered polite nods, others murmured vague questions.

"Such a shock, huh?"

"She didn't seem like the type…"

"Do you think it was really… you know?"

Each time, I gave the same neutral response. "We're still looking into everything." Then I'd excuse myself and move on.

I also received several looks, too many to count. Some were heavy with grief, others hollowed out by confusion. But a few? A few were sharper. Accusing, suspicious, like I knew more than I was saying. Like maybe I was part of whatever people were whispering about behind the scenes.

The same looks I'd been seeing more often around town lately, at the grocery store, at stop signs, through barely cracked windows. People talk, they always have. But now it felt different, more charged. Like they weren't just questioning what happened to Mara… they were questioning who they trusted.

When you wear a badge in a small town, that trust is everything.

I expected it, but it still stung. Some of the people throwing those glances were folks I'd helped through tragedies of their own. People whose hands I'd held in the worst moments of their lives. Now they looked at me like I was on the wrong side of something. Like maybe I was protecting someone. Covering for Reid, or maybe… covering for myself.

It made me wonder, when this is all said and done, when the last interview is finished, the last search warrant filed, and whatever truth is hiding finally steps into the light, where do we go from here? Not just me, but the whole department. The whole damn town.

Whatever Mara's death uncovers, I don't think this community will ever be the same. Some things break and can be repaired; others change shape completely. This felt like the latter.

I couldn't shake the feeling that I was changing too.

But my eyes kept drifting toward the door.

I was waiting for her.

Crystal.

When she finally arrived, it was like a spark across dry grass. Subtle, but you could feel the room react. Heads turned, whispers fluttered like moths. She came alone, no husband beside her, just a small clutch in her hand and uncertainty in her step.

She wore black, not flashy, not defiant, just enough to say, "I'm here." But her presence was loud in a room full of quiet grief.

I watched her eyes scan the space. She saw Reid, hesitated. Then she saw me. Our gaze locked for a split second before she looked away and joined the line.

I moved closer, not too close, not obvious, but enough to observe. The interactions mattered now. Who greeted her, who avoided her, who whispered after she passed. These were the human fingerprints on a still-warm story.

One of Mara's sisters, I assumed by the resemblance, stood stiffly as Crystal offered a quiet word. The woman didn't respond, just stared at her until Crystal moved on.

Crystal reached the casket and paused. Her eyes flicked up to Mara's face, then down again. She whispered something I couldn't hear and brushed her fingers along the edge of the wood. Then she stepped away, face unreadable, and moved toward an empty chair near the side wall.

I joined her a few minutes later, slipping into the seat beside her.

"You came," I said quietly.

"I had to," she replied. "Even if no one wanted me here."

"Doesn't matter what they want. This is part of it now."

She didn't respond right away. Her eyes stayed on the casket, her jaw set.

"I keep thinking… if I hadn't gotten involved,"

"You don't get to own that kind of guilt alone," I interrupted gently. "Whatever this is, it started long before you."

She looked at me then, really looked. "Do you think he did it?"

The question hit hard because she wasn't asking for show. She wanted to believe he couldn't. Needed to.

"I think we're still figuring it out," I said. "And who Mara really was, too."

Crystal blinked slowly, then turned her attention back to the front of the room. Reid was still in his place, greeting more guests, his face fixed in a perfect mask of mourning.

The cracks were subtle, but they were there.

As the night wrapped up, I could see the exhaustion on Reid and the boys. It's been a long hard week and today by itself was a long hard day with hundreds of people filing through.

Sue and I approached Reid, "You good"

"Ya heading home, need rest"

"You or the boys need anything? Something to eat we can grab it and bring it over"

"Ya you know that would be great"

"Ok, Pizza?"

"Sure"

Me and Sue ordered a few pizzas, expecting some family to stop by after the wake, and they did. Quiet, slow-moving, the kind of worn-out grief that makes people speak in half-sentences and nods. Most of them were unfamiliar to me, Mara's people. Her sister, her mother, a couple of cousins maybe. They'd come in from out of town, the ones she'd left behind when she built a life here with Reid.

This was the first time I really watched them interact with him.

It was civil, polite even. But there was a weight in the room that hadn't been there earlier at the funeral home. Small talk fell flat, thank yous for the pizza, soft murmurs about the boys, an occasional glance around the living room. But nothing close to warmth, nothing close to trust.

Reid kept busy or at least looked like he was. Moving paper plates from counter to table. Getting drinks from the fridge. Talking, but never really *connecting*. He seemed to know exactly where he stood with them.

I watched Mara's sister especially. Her posture was stiff, her voice clipped when she spoke to Reid. I couldn't help but wonder how much she knew, or thought she knew. It didn't take long to figure out that something unspoken was hanging heavy between them. There were no accusations, but there was no affection either.

And Crystal? She didn't show.

That silence was louder than any confrontation. I had half-expected her to come by, maybe out of guilt or habit. But her absence confirmed what I'd already sensed at the funeral home: she knew she wasn't welcome. Mara's sister hadn't looked at her once back there. Didn't speak her name, didn't need to.

They knew.

Or they suspected enough to draw their own conclusions.

Sooner or later, I'd need to talk to them, especially the sister. The way she watched Reid, the way she didn't, those are the moments that stick in investigations. She might have insights no one else could give me. A version of Mara's life that Reid couldn't spin.

I found a quiet moment, just after people had finished eating and the room settled into hushed conversation. Sue was by my side, and I took that as my cue. We made our way toward Mara's sister, who was sitting near the fireplace with a paper plate balanced on her lap, mostly untouched. Her eyes flicked up as we approached, guarded but not cold.

"Hi," I said gently. "I'm sorry to intrude. I just wanted to introduce myself. I'm,"

"You're the officer," she said. Her voice wasn't sharp, but it wasn't warm either.

"I am," I nodded. "But I'm also a friend. This is my wife, Sue."

Tracy's face softened just a touch as she shook Sue's hand.

"We just wanted to say how sorry we are," Sue said. "Mara meant a lot to both of us."

"She was… everything," Tracy replied, her voice catching for the first time. "I still can't believe it."

I shared a quick memory of Mara, the kind of small-town anecdote that brings a smile without too much weight. Tracy laughed faintly, that bittersweet kind of laugh that disappears almost as quickly as it comes. She added a memory of her own, something about Mara sneaking out of the house when they were teens, and for a few moments it felt like we were just people sharing grief.

But I couldn't ignore the reason behind everything. The things that hadn't been said. The questions hanging in the air.

"I don't want to take up your time tonight," I said, lowering my voice just slightly, "but if you have a few minutes before you leave town… I'd really like to talk. Just to get to know Mara better, the real her."

She looked at me for a long moment. Not suspicious, but wary, measuring.

"You think something happened, don't you?" she asked quietly.

"I think there's more to understand," I replied, careful with my words.

She nodded slowly. "Okay. I'll be at the inn where we're staying. We've got the funeral tomorrow, but… how about in the morning? Before everything?"

"Absolutely. Just name the time."

"Eight?"

"Eight works."

"Okay," she said, almost to herself. Then, after a pause, "Thank you for coming tonight, it means something, even if none of this makes sense."

I nodded once. "It will, one way or another."

She looked away, blinking back whatever was trying to surface, and I let her have the moment. Sue and I stepped away to give her space, but I kept thinking about her question, about whether I believed something had happened.

The truth was, I didn't know what I believed anymore. But I knew one thing: the answers were still out there, and I had a feeling Tracy held more than a few of them.

Chapter Eight

It was a beautiful, warm fall morning, the kind that would normally make you want to open every window and let the breeze carry the smell of leaves and coffee through the house. But not today.

Sue and I arrived early. I pulled into a spot near the back of the lot, turned the engine off, and just sat there. Hands still on the wheel. Eyes locked on nothing. I don't even know what I was thinking, if I was thinking at all. Everything felt muted. Like grief had its own weather system, pressing in from all sides.

Sue placed her hand on my arm gently, "Are we going in?" she asked.

I didn't answer at first, I couldn't. The fog in my chest was too thick. She asked again, this time her voice softer, like she was pulling me out of something deep.

That's when it really set in.

Mara was gone, really gone.

This wasn't just a case anymore. Wasn't just another scene or report or investigation to file. This was someone we loved someone Sue shared coffee and late-night texts with. Someone whose boys had played in our backyard with ours. Someone who filled the corners of our lives in the ways you don't notice until they're gone.

We stepped out of the car. I adjusted my collar out of habit. Sue reached for my hand, and I gripped it tighter than I meant to. Her fingers laced into mine like a lifeline.

Inside the church, the air smelled like flowers and old wood and every funeral I'd ever been to. That scent always turned my stomach, it was thick with finality.

The pews creaked as people sat. I could feel eyes on me, some nods. some glances that looked away too fast. Others... lingered, judgmental, suspicious. I wasn't just a friend or a guest anymore, I was the guy who was supposed to know what happened. Maybe the guy who didn't do enough.

Reid sat at the front with the boys. They clung to him like life rafts. Tracy sat on the opposite side, her posture stiff, her jaw clenched. The space between them wasn't just physical, it was emotional, hollow, and wide as a canyon. You could feel it.

I glanced at Sue beside me. Her lips were tight, eyes red but dry. She had loved Mara in the way women love their closest friends, quietly, deeply, with unspoken understanding. This was hitting her harder than she let on. She'd been strong for the boys, strong for me, but I could feel the cracks in her stillness. She squeezed my hand again and didn't let go.

The minister began. "We're here today to celebrate the life of Mara Michelle Carrington…"

I barely heard him. My mind kept drifting, back to the morning coffee shop with Tracy, to the questions she asked, to the doubt I still carried. But more than that, I kept feeling this ache in my chest that wasn't just professional. It was personal. It was a breaking I didn't know how to mend.

The organ swelled with "Amazing Grace." I heard Sue sniff beside me, a small sharp sound that cut deeper than the music. I reached across the program I was crushing in my hand and rested my palm on her knee. She covered it with hers.

Later, after the service, I found Reid receiving people in the narthex, the boys pressed close. His face looked worn to the bone. I said what I could, offered the usual words. He nodded, but his eyes stayed distant. Hollow, I couldn't tell what was behind them, pain, guilt, confusion. Maybe all three.

When Sue and I got back to the car, I sat behind the wheel again, staring out the windshield.

She finally broke the silence. "What are you thinking?"

I looked at her, she already knew the answer. But she let me say it anyway.

"I don't know yet."

She exhaled, then said quietly, "He's grieving, I saw it. That wasn't fake."

"I know," I said.

"I also know you won't stop digging," she added.

She was right.

She was worried, not just for the case. For me.

We didn't talk much on the drive home, we didn't need to. She placed her hand on my thigh as I drove, her thumb tracing slow, steady circles. A small, steady comfort in a day filled with sharp edges.

I dropped her off and kissed her cheek. She touched my face like she was memorizing it. "Be careful," she said. "With all of it, especially with yourself."

Then I turned the car toward the station. Because I couldn't sit in the stillness, not yet.

Now that the formalities were over, the wake, the funeral, the polite condolences, I could finally shift into what I knew: work. Grief still lingered like fog, but the investigator in me was sharpening again.

It was time to find the truth and protect what was left of the people I cared about, especially the ones who didn't know they needed protecting.

I sat at my desk, notepad in hand, and began building my list. One name after another. As I wrote, my memory flickered through the faces I had seen at the wake, in the church pews, lingering quietly at the cemetery. Some had barely made eye contact. Others had stayed too long, said too little, or said too much. Every glance, every exchange, every absence had meaning now.

Even if it was just to ask a simple question, "When did you last see her?" or "Did you notice anything different?", they were going on the list. No interaction was too small to revisit. The truth had a way of hiding in the mundane.

I also needed to loop in Jack. He and I would need to split the load, work many of these conversations one-on-one. But more importantly, we had to be in sync, fully transparent, every detail shared, every instinct checked. This wasn't the time for pride or assumptions. This case was growing, deeper than we thought. If there were cracks forming beneath the surface, we had to be the ones to spot them, together.

Tomorrow, the real work begins.

Chapter Nine

Back at the station, the morning kicked off faster than I expected. The first thing waiting for me was a message from the State Technical Lab. The tech there wanted to send me the phone log results, months' worth, he said, but didn't want to just drop them in my inbox. "You need to be present when you receive this," the message read. That could mean anything, volume, sensitivity, or both. I replied to confirm I was ready, and that I'd be watching for the email.

No sooner had I stood up from my desk than I saw Stephen pulling into the lot. His truck door opened slowly, and he stepped out carrying a zippered bag, gray canvas, school-issued. I opened the station door before he could knock.

"Here it is," he said, holding it out.

"The phone?"

"Yup."

"Great. Thank you," I said, taking the bag. I could feel the weight of it, not just the physical device, but whatever it might hold inside.

Before I could turn back inside, Stephen paused. "I also went through the school's internal email system this morning," he said, glancing over his shoulder like he didn't want to be overheard. "I've got access to all staff accounts, and... well, there are several emails between Reid and Crystal. You're going to want to see them."

"You're sure they're personal?" I asked, already knowing the answer by the look on his face.

"They don't start that way," he said. "But they drift. You'll see."

"Absolutely," I nodded. "Send them over as soon as you can."

"I'll be back at the school in an hour or so. You'll have them today."

I thanked him again, watching him walk back to his truck. For a small-town school principal, Stephen was being incredibly cooperative, and smart. He knew what this could mean for the district, and for his people. I respected that.

Back inside, I placed the phone bag on my desk next to my notes and powered up my laptop. Between the logs coming in from the tech lab and this new data from the school, it felt like the fog might finally start to lift.

Or it was about to get a whole lot thicker.

The email from the State Technical Lab came through just before noon. No subject line, just a long string of characters in the file name and a brief message: *"As discussed, here are the full log results. Let me know if you need help parsing anything."*

I clicked the attachment but didn't open it.

Not here.

I needed absolute quiet, no phones ringing, no questions from the team, no casual knock on my office door from someone meaning well. I needed space to read every line, catch every timestamp, look for the small things, the inconsistencies, the calls that didn't fit, the patterns no one else would notice on a first pass.

So, I packed up my laptop and headed home. Told dispatch I'd be working remote for the afternoon and left no room for questions. This wasn't something I could delegate or rush. I needed to give it my full attention.

Once at home, I set up at the dining room table. Sue was out; the house was silent. Just me, the glow of the screen, and a slow, steady unravelling of digital breadcrumbs. These logs, phone calls, text timestamps, tower pings, they weren't just data. They were a timeline. A window into choices, conversations, secrets.

I didn't want to miss a thing.

At first, I spent hours just scanning, trying to find the earliest email between them. I wanted to build a timeline, understand where it all began. The first few messages were exactly what you'd expect: strictly professional, short replies about scheduling meetings, safety protocols, updates on staff.

But even in those early exchanges, there was something… warm. Friendly. A little too personal for colleagues who barely knew each other.

Then, as I followed the thread forward, it became clearer. Subtle shifts at first, compliments, inside jokes, little comments that had nothing to do with work. Then came longer emails, late at night, confessions about stress at home, frustrations with their spouses. It wasn't cynical, not even sneaky. It was two people slowly stepping into something they didn't, or wouldn't, pull back from.

Eventually, the tone changed, it turned. The flirtation gave way to boldness. The messages grew more intimate. Then blunt, sex talk, graphic, unfiltered. Then came photos, then videos.

There was no shame between them, just a sense of urgency. I'm sure, positive, they never thought anyone else would ever see these. Certainly not me, not law enforcement, not anyone outside their little bubble.

But now here I was, wading through it all like some unwanted voyeur, parsing emotional breadcrumbs and private fantasies for truth, motive, and evidence.

No matter how uncomfortable it made me, I kept going. Because somewhere in this chain was a window into what Reid was thinking. Who he really was when no one was looking. Maybe, even if he never wrote the words outright, what he was capable of.

Once I had all the emails and texts in chronological order, I turned my focus to the night Mara died.

That timeline mattered. It had to.

At 11:30 PM, Reid sent Crystal a message:
"I'll be leaving soon, can I stop by?"
No reply.

Then, at 11:45 PM, another:
"Hey babe, you up?"
Still nothing.

At exactly midnight, he texted again:
"I'm leaving, guess you're sleeping. Talk tomorrow babe."

Then, at 12:20 AM, Crystal responded:
"Hey Hun, I'm up now. Sorry. You still there?"

Reid replied almost instantly:
"Just walked in my house. Hold on, see what I can do."

I read it twice. Then again. It was subtle, but it hit me hard.

"See what I can do."

It wasn't just casual late-night chatter; it sounded like a pivot. Like a plan changing. Like someone trying to manage a situation.

It narrowed a window I needed to define. Mara was gone shortly before or after that text, before Reid ever set foot in that house… or maybe just as he did.

Everything about those messages begged to be read between the lines. Every word felt like a breadcrumb left behind by people who thought no one would ever retrace their steps.

But I was retracing them now. Every single one.

At **12:25 AM**, Reid replied to Crystal:
"Ok, on my way. I have a few minutes."
Crystal responded almost immediately:
"OK, awesome."

Then, at **12:50 AM**, Mara texted Reid.
"Any idea when you'll be home? I'm waiting."

That hit me like a weight. She was still up. Still expecting him.

At **12:55 AM**, Reid responded:
"Sorry, got tied up at PD. On my way in a minute."

But then came the part that stopped me cold.

At **1:30 AM**, a full **thirty-five minutes later**, Reid texted Crystal again:
"Ok, home. Goodnight."

Crystal sent back a simple 🩶 **emoji**.
End of conversation.

But the timing didn't add up. Reid had told me he was gone for 15–20 minutes after getting home. If that was true, this text exchange was over an hour later than it should've been.

Where was he during that gap, looks like with Crystal? More importantly, was Mara still awake and waiting for him when he got home? If so, why hadn't she messaged again? What happened when he got home?

Something wasn't right.

Did he ever go to the PD. He was out longer than he admitted, and the messages proved it.
That window of time, from 12:25 to 1:30 AM, mattered now more than ever. Because somewhere inside it, the truth about what happened to Mara might be hiding. I also noted another interesting text, at 7:22 AM the morning Mara died, at about that time Reid would have been in the ambulance heading to the hospital as the crew in the back performed lifesaving efforts on his wife. He texted Crystal, "on the way to hospital, Its Mara It's not good", Crystal replied several times trying to get more information, and Reid didn't respond until early afternoon at about the time he was heading back home. He called crystal for a 9 min conversation.

I didn't find any texts from Reid that could be interpreted as plotting or suggesting any plan to "get Mara out of the way." Nothing direct, nothing that felt like a smoking gun. But I did find something else, something that lingered.

There was one message from Crystal, buried in the middle of a long text thread, where she wrote:
"I wish he would die."

It was in reference to her own husband. The tone read like venting, frustration boiling over in a private moment. Reid didn't acknowledge the comment at all. No reaction, no follow-up, no fuel to that fire. He moved the conversation in a different direction.

Still, it sat with me.

There were other conversations, too, talks of the future, of being together, of being free. The same things Crystal described in her earlier interview. Fantasies, plans, at least in their heads. Enough to make the whole thing feel deeper, more real, more dangerous.

It's time I talk to Crystal again.

This time, I'm going to her home. She's a witness, not a suspect. I want her comfortable. I want her relaxed. I need her to talk freely. But I'm also prepared, if it comes to it, to remind her what I know. The photos. The videos. The words they exchanged in the dark. I'll shame her with them if I must.

But I'm hoping I don't.

First, Jack and I need to meet and catch up. I gave him a call, and we agreed to meet at the PD at 7 p.m. tonight. It's important we're completely aligned, no gaps, no missed threads. I've been buried in these messages for hours, and he needs to see them for himself, with his own eyes and instincts. I also have the batch of school emails Stephen forwarded ones I haven't even had time to go through yet. I'll hand those off to Jack too. Between the two of us, we'll start to connect more of the puzzle, piece by piece.

Chapter Ten

I decided to meet with Crystal alone this time, no uniform, no cruiser. I dressed casually, just me and my thoughts. This wasn't an official visit. At least, not on the surface.

She opened the door with a curious expression.
"I was wondering who was pulling in," she said.
"Yeah… I didn't want any interruptions. Figured I'd swing by when I wasn't on patrol."
"Well, okay, come on in then. In that case, you want a drink?"
"Um… sure. What do you have?"
"Bourbon."
"Alright. On the rocks. Thanks."

She disappeared into the kitchen and returned with a glass of bourbon for me and a glass of wine for herself. We sat in the living room, just the two of us, a soft hum of silence between us.

She crossed one leg over the other and offered a half-smile.
"So, what brings you back?"

I took a slow sip, let the burn settle.
"There are still some holes I need to fill," I said, my eyes meeting hers. "I'm hoping you can help me with that."

"Ok, sure, whatever you need," Crystal said, settling back, her voice a little too casual.

"When did you first hear about Mara's suicide?"

"Umm… let's see. It must've been at church. Someone mentioned it, and the priest said a prayer."

"What time was that service?"

"11:00 AM."

"Did you have any indication before that, earlier that morning, that something serious had happened with Mara?"

She hesitated, eyes flicking away. "Well…" she started sheepishly, "yeah. Reid texted me something strange. Said he was heading to the hospital with Mara. That something had happened."

"Do you know where he was texting from?"

"No, not really. I just figured… his car?"

"Would it surprise you if I told you he was texting you from inside the ambulance?"

Her head snapped slightly, eyes searching mine. "Um… no, I guess not. I mean… he's an EMT."

"You're not surprised that while EMTs were performing CPR on his wife, trying to save her life, he was thinking about texting you?"

She looked down, caught off guard. Silence. Her face tightened as she searched for something to say. I didn't press. I liked that she was on her heels.

"Ok," I said, calmly, shifting gears, "let's step back a little. Let's talk about the night before. Early morning. Before all this."

She took a deep breath, clearly trying to recompose herself. She even forced a smile, but it didn't hold.

"Did Reid work that night, the night before Mara died?"

"I'm not sure," she said quickly. "I don't keep his schedule."

"Ok, Crystal, listen," I said, tone sharpening. "Let's assume I know more than you think I do, because I do. These aren't random questions. I'm asking them for a reason. Now think again… Did Reid work that night?"

She nodded, quietly. "Yes… yes, he did."

"Do you know when his shift ended?"

"About midnight."

"How do you know that?"

She paused. "He was texting me. He wanted to come see me. He texted a few times, but I was sleeping."

"Did you answer him?"

"Yes. I woke up just after midnight and responded."

"Then what?"

"He said he just got home. Told me to give him a minute."

"What does that mean, 'give me a minute'?"

"Well…" she looked away again, "he ended up coming over. So, I guess that meant he came up with a story to leave the house."

"Did he tell you anything about what was going on at home? Anything at all?"

"No," she said, quickly. "Not at all. I asked, but… he said nothing."

"So, Reid came over, here? To this house?"

"Yes."

"I thought you didn't move in here until after everything happened?"

"I didn't," she said, a little defensive. "But we've had this house for a while. We used to rent it out."

"So, you were spending nights here before the separation?"

She nodded. "Yeah… we weren't getting along. It was easier."

"Was this the first time Reid came here?"

"No," she said quickly. "He's been here several times."

"Do you think anyone saw him?"

"I doubt it," she said, glancing out the window. "As you can see, you can't see the house or the driveway from the road."

I let the silence stretch for a beat.

"So, what did you and Reid do… that night?"

She took a breath, her voice flat. "We had sex," she said. "That's why he came over."

No hesitation, no shame, just fact.

"Is that what the relationship was? Just sex?" I asked, keeping my tone steady. "Or was there talk about a future?"

She shook her head immediately. "It was… it is more than that. We love each other. We're going to be together."

"So, you expected that he was leaving Mara?"

"Yes. Absolutely."

"Was that discussed that night?" I watched her closely. "Did you press him? Point out that you were already separated, and now he needed to do the same?"

She hesitated, then gave a small shrug. "Okay… maybe a little. I wasn't threatening or anything, just… pointing out facts."

"What was his response?"

"He said he was working on it. Waiting for the right time."

"Did that answer satisfy you?"

She looked down at her glass. "No. But I didn't push it after that."

"Did he know you weren't happy with that answer?"

"I'm pretty sure," she said. "I'm not exactly great at hiding how I feel."

There was a moment of silence. Then her eyes snapped up to meet mine, wide and unsteady.

"Wait, you don't think… you're not saying that me pressuring him made something happen that night? No. No, I didn't push him that hard. He couldn't… he wouldn't do that. I'm sure. I *know* him."

I didn't answer right away. I just let her words sit there between us, uncertain and trembling. Because now, *she* was questioning it too.

OK thank you, thank you for the bourbon and thank you for your cooperation and I must insist you don't communicate with Reid in any way, direct or indirect. OK?

"Yes, I understand"

As I drove away, I realized it's time to brief the Chief on all issues we have found to this point.

The next morning, Jack and I sat down with the Chief. He'd been asking for a briefing, pressure was building, not just from town chatter but from the Town Board itself. People were talking, people were *watching*. The Chief didn't want this cloud hanging over the department much longer.

He kicked off the meeting before we even opened our folders.

"Listen," he said, palms flat on the table. "Reid's a good guy, always has been. This is a tragedy, an awful one. Yeah, maybe he had an affair. Poor judgment, sure, but people make mistakes. I don't see the value in dragging this out or beating the same horse more than once."

His tone was calm, but I knew what it was underneath: exhaustion. Concern for the department's reputation. Concern for *his* position. Maybe, a little personal bias, because we all *knew* Reid. Worked next to him. Trusted him.

"I hear you, Chief," I said, keeping my voice respectful but firm. "But can we walk you through what we've found so far? There are still serious concerns we need to address."

He leaned back and folded his arms. "Alright. Go ahead. Lay it out for me. Let's see if we can answer these issues and move forward."

Jack and I exchanged a glance. This was the moment. The point where the case either died in a file folder or cracked wide open under the weight of inconvenient truth.

Jack opened his notebook, flipped to the right page, and nodded at me.

"Alright," I began. "We'll keep it direct. First, timeline inconsistencies. The night Mara died, Reid claimed he left the PD and came straight home and then ran back to the PD to check the front door. But texts between him and Crystal show he made a stop, *at her house*, for nearly an hour before coming back. That puts him away from the house during a crucial window. Mara was still alive when he left."

The Chief frowned, but didn't interrupt.

"Second," Jack jumped in, "the tone and content of those messages. We recovered texts and emails that show a romantic and sexual relationship between Reid and Crystal. Fine adults make choices. But that night, Crystal confirmed they had sex. She says he left her place just before 1:30AM. Mara texted him *during that time*, asking when he was coming home. He lied to her, said he was at the PD. That's not grief, it's concealment."

I added, "There's more. Crystal admitted she pressured Reid that night, said he needed to leave Mara just like she left her husband. She asked if he was ready to move forward. That's a lot of emotional weight just hours before Mara ends up dead."

The Chief rubbed his chin and glanced at the ceiling. "You saying she pushed him into it?"

"No," I said. "But it adds motive, opportunity, and pressure. We're not accusing yet, but we're also not ignoring the storm that was brewing in that house."

Jack flipped to another page. "Then there's the digital forensics. The state tech lab sent us Reid's phone logs, and we found no messages indicating a plot or plan, but the volume and timing of communication between him and Crystal is alarming. More than a dozen messages that night, right up until just after Mara's death. The last text from Reid to Crystal? 'Ok home, goodnight.' Sent at 1:30AM., when Reid said he was home by 12:40 AM"

That hit the table hard.

The Chief looked down, jaw tight. "That's 50 minutes."

"Exactly," I said. "Why did he lie and say he was home earlier? What did he find when he walked in?"

There was a long silence.

The Chief tapped his fingers on the table slowly. "Anything else?"

"One more thing," I said. "Crystal initially claimed she didn't know about the death until she heard it at church the next morning. But she admitted, under light pressure, that Reid texted her earlier, saying he was taking Mara to the hospital. He sent that while EMTs were still doing CPR. He was in the ambulance. That level of detachment, texting his mistress while his wife's dying... it's concerning."

"It's damning," Jack muttered.

I nodded. "We're not saying Reid did anything yet, Chief. But we're saying there's enough here to keep this open. To keep digging. We're asking for your support." "We need to talk to Reid again, his first stories are not adding up"

The Chief leaned back in his chair, arms crossed, eyes focused somewhere past us. For a long moment, he didn't say a word. The silence wasn't uncomfortable, just heavy. Calculating.

Finally, he exhaled through his nose and nodded slowly.

"Alright," he said. "This is... more than I thought. A hell of a lot more."

He glanced at Jack, then at me. "You're right not to let it go, we owe it to her, to Mara and to the community, even if they don't know it yet."

He rubbed his forehead and sat forward again, resting his elbows on the table. "This doesn't look good. Not for Reid. Not for us as a department. But burying this doesn't make it go away; it just makes it fester."

He gave us a tired but firm look. "You two keep digging. Quietly. Methodically. No leaks. I'll handle the Board, and the public noise. If they want to yell, they can yell at me."

Jack gave a quick nod. I sat back slightly, tension I didn't even realize I was holding finally easing just a notch.

"Let me be clear," the Chief added. "I still hope this isn't what it looks like. But I'm not going to stand in the way if it is. Keep me looped in. If anything breaks big, if we're about to cross the line from internal suspicions to a full criminal case, I need to be the first to know."

"Of course," I said.

He stood, signalling we were done. "Whatever this turns out to be… finish it right. All the way through."

Chapter Eleven

I decided to check the burner phone I'd given Reid. I had it set up so all texts would forward directly to me. Since last night, after my conversation with Crystal, Reid had texted her multiple times, each time with no reply. That was a relief. No sign he was catching on yet.

But for how long?

The silence from Crystal could be the calm before the storm. If Reid caught wind that we were closing in, everything could change. He hasn't lawyered up yet, but I knew that moment was looming. That's the thing about men like Reid, pride, fear, denial, they all churn together until one breaks the surface.

If he does, and sticks to his story about what happened that night in the house and the garage, how could we prove otherwise? The text messages, the emails, the photos and videos, they told a story that didn't line up with his version. But without concrete proof tying it all together, it was just smoke.

We needed to find the spark.

I pulled into Crystal's driveway, gravel crunching under the tires. The late afternoon sun filtered through overhanging branches, casting shifting shadows across the worn wood porch and the scattered flowerpots. She stepped outside almost immediately, arms already crossed, as if she'd been watching for me. Her expression was guarded but tired, like a woman who'd been fighting a silent war for too long.

"What's up?" she asked, voice low but steady, a little wary.

"I haven't talked to Reid at all," she added quickly, like a defense before I could even ask. Her eyes flickered with something I couldn't place, fear, maybe? Or suspicion?

"Okay, good. Thank you," I said. "But I'm here because I need your help."

She narrowed her eyes, shoulders stiffening. "Like… what do you need now?"

I took a breath, grounding myself. "I need to get the truth out of Reid. The story he's giving us about what happened in the house that night, it doesn't add up. I can't verify any of it. That's where you come in."

Her arms tightened across her chest, the sudden defensiveness like a shield. "What exactly is he saying?"

I studied her reaction as I answered. "He's claiming that when he got home, Mara wanted to go out to the van and have sex, like they used to. He says they did, then he went upstairs, fell asleep, and woke up to find her in the garage… with the van running."

Crystal blinked, her expression shifting from disbelief to something rawer hurt, maybe even rage. "He's saying that happened? That they… hooked up that night?"

"Yeah," I nodded, "That's his version. There's no one else who can say what really happened in that house that's the problem. But maybe you can help us get there."

She looked away toward the trees, mouth tightening, then turned back, eyes sharp. "Wait. He said they had sex that night?"

"That's what he told us."

Her jaw dropped. "He told me they don't even kiss anymore. What the fuck is he doing to me?" Her voice rose, fury overtaking disbelief. "He's lying to everyone."

I stepped in gently. "Crystal, listen to me. You can't help us if you let the anger take over. You want the truth, right? Just like we do?"

She nodded slowly, still fuming but trying to steady herself. Her hands unclenched, and I saw the exhaustion beneath the fire.

"Then let's find it, together."

"Okay," she said finally, exhaling hard like she was blowing the anger out of her system. "What's the plan?"

I kept my voice calm, deliberate. "First, answer his texts. Apologize, tell him your phone was acting up or broken, whatever feels natural. Keep it light. If he asks whether we came to talk, just say yeah, but that it wasn't anything big."

She nodded slowly, eyes narrowing in thought. "So, play it cool."

"Exactly. We don't want to spook him. We want him talking, and if he thinks everything's still safe between you two, he'll open up. He's more honest when he's not being watched."

"What happens after that?" she asked, her voice softer now, a thread of fear weaving through.

"We wait, let's see what he says. If he keeps reaching out, we find the right moment. Maybe it's a call, maybe it's a meet-up, but we'll guide it. When that happens, you'll know exactly what to do."

Crystal looked at me for a long moment, then nodded again, this time with purpose.

"I'll do it. I want to know the truth too. If he's been lying to me and everyone else this whole time…" She trailed off, shaking her head, eyes glossy with unshed tears.

I didn't have to say anything more. The trap was starting to take shape, and now we had bait. I asked her to keep it simple the next few days, try not to see him, put it off as much as you can. I will be back in touch soon.

That night, I couldn't sleep. The house was too quiet, my mind too loud. I stayed up reviewing call logs and rereading messages from Reid's burner phone. I kept thinking about Crystal, whether she was really in this with me or just playing along until she cracked. I pictured her sitting on that porch, trying to steady her breath, wondering if she'd made the right choice.

I imagined the first conversation she'd have with him. The one where she finally responded. Would she be calm? Act confused? Pretend nothing happened? She had to hit just the right tone, make him feel safe, even missed. That's what would get him to open up.

I thought about calling in a favor with a judge I used to work closely with, maybe find a way to get a warrant anyway. But without the Chief's approval, it could cost me. My career, my badge. I wasn't ready to burn it all down unless I was certain.

We needed something stronger. Something that tied Reid directly to motive and opportunity.

First, we needed to talk to Mara's sister. I needed a better picture of Mara's state of mind lately.

I gave her a call. She was still in town, and we agreed to meet at the beachside park along the lake. Quiet, out of the way. A good place to talk.

When I arrived, the late afternoon light cast a golden glow over the calm water, shimmering faintly as the breeze ruffled the surface. The smell of water and damp earth filled the air. It was peaceful here, so different from the storm swirling inside me.

She was already there when I walked up, sitting on a weathered bench, legs crossed, looking out across the water. Her posture was tense but open, like someone holding a fragile secret.

Once we sat down, I got right to it.

"I know you spoke to Mara about three days before she passed," I said. "But before that, how often were you two in touch?"

She nodded, thoughtful. "We usually talked at least once a week, but... you know how life is. Sometimes a few weeks would go by."

"Yeah, I get that," I said. "Over the past few months, did you notice any changes in her?"

She looked out at the lake, eyes tracing the ripples. "I've been thinking about that a lot since she died. Wondering if I missed something... or didn't listen close enough. The only thing that really stands out now is, she talked about Dad a few times this year."

"Specifically, what?"

"Well, the anniversary came up. We always acknowledge it. But this time, she had more questions. She talked more about what she remembered. She was ten when it happened."

"Can you tell me more about your dad's suicide? I'm not sure I ever heard the full story."

She nodded slowly. "I was thirteen. I don't remember every detail, but… me and Mara woke up to Mom screaming outside. We ran to our bedroom window and saw a neighbor pulling Dad out of the back door of his car. There was smoke coming out, and I remember seeing a hose on the ground near the door."

She paused, the memory clearly vivid despite the years. Her hands clenched tightly in her lap.

"Dad was lying on the ground. Mom was yelling at him to wake up. Then the ambulance and police arrived. The ambulance took him to the hospital, but… it was too late."

I sat with that for a moment, the image sinking in. The quiet lapping of the lake felt distant, like the world kept spinning while she carried that pain.

"Mara saw all of that?"

"Yeah," she said, eyes still fixed on the horizon. "She did."

I listened carefully as she spoke, letting the silence settle around us once she finished. The waves from the lake rolled gently in the background, steady and rhythmic, nothing like the chaos she was describing.

"So, the hose was connected to the exhaust?" I asked softly.

She nodded, eyes distant. "It was on the ground, Dad parked in front of the house, passenger side facing the house. Ran a hose from the tailpipe through the window or side door, something like that. That's what I was told. What I remember is seeing the hose on the ground… and the smoke."

"Mara saw that too?" I asked quietly.

"She did. I don't think she ever forgot it, even though she was only ten. I mean… how do you forget something like that?" Her voice cracked slightly.

"Who told you that Mara he had passed?"

"My mom. When she came back from the hospital."

"How was she?"

"Upset. Frantic. Crying, but madder than anything else. She seemed… angry at him. She just said it bluntly: that Dad had committed suicide. That he ran a hose from the car exhaust into the car, got drunk, and fell asleep until the fumes killed him."

"How did you and Mara take it?"

"I think we were already crying by then. Probably because we saw him go in the ambulance and because Mom was falling apart. But the reality of it?" She shook her head slowly. "I don't think it sank in for either of us for hours."

I took a moment. "Did she ever bring it up before this year?"

"No. Not really. That's what's strange. It was like she had compartmentalized it for years… and then, this spring, it was like she needed to understand it. She asked about little things, what I remembered, what Mom said, even if we ever thought Dad was pushed into it."

"Did she ever talk about wanting to hurt herself?" I asked carefully.

"No. Never. I mean… she struggled sometimes, like we all do. But she always had a sense of purpose. Her job, her friends… Reid." She paused. "Actually, now that I think about it, she used to talk about them all the time. But the last few times? She barely mentioned him."

I noted that. "Did she seem distant?"

"Yeah. I thought maybe they were just going through a phase. But when she didn't talk about him… it wasn't frustration. It felt more like," She searched for the word. ", acceptance. Like she had already emotionally stepped away."

"That's important," I said, "and the way her father died, same method, same setup, it's hard to ignore that."

She looked over sharply. "Wait… are you saying she copied it?"

I held her gaze. "I'm saying… it doesn't feel right. The similarities to your dad's death, it could be staged by anybody."

Her face went pale. She wrapped her arms around herself; eyes locked on the lake.

"You think someone made it look that way?" she whispered.

I nodded slowly. "Not for sure but that's what I'm trying to find out. That's why every detail matters."

She was quiet for a long time. Then she said softly, "If he did this… if Reid had anything to do with it, I hope you catch him. I hope he doesn't see it coming."

"My gut says he didn't, and this was a suicide, but I can't ignore red flags, I have to have all the answers as best as I can" and "He won't get off, if he did" I said. "But I need your help, to make sure of that."

The lake shimmered under the sun. But all I could see were shadows.

Chapter Twelve

Jack was able to secure a meeting with Mara's therapist. It wasn't easy, apparently, no one even knew she was seeing anyone. She had gone out of her way to keep it secret, driving 45 minutes away just to talk to someone.

It was a cold, rainy morning as Jack and I headed over to meet the therapist. The weather matched the mood, grey, heavy, uncertain. It also gave me and Jack a rare moment together, just the two of us. We hadn't had a real conversation in days. We'd both been chasing down different threads, me on Crystal and Reid, and Jack deep-diving into Mara's work life.

On the drive over, he filled me in on what he'd found.

"I met with several of her coworkers," he began, rubbing the fog off the inside of the windshield. "None of them seemed to know what was really going on with her. She was friendly, talked a lot about the boys, bragged about them, really. But nobody said she opened up about anything personal."

He paused, glancing at me. "A few of them did say she'd changed, though. That she wasn't quite the same lately. Still smiled, still kind, still good with the patients… but quieter. Like something was fading in her."

"Did anyone have any clue she was in that much pain?" I asked.

Jack shook his head. "No one saw this coming, not even close. They were stunned, completely blindsided. Said she gave no signs of being in a dark place. But… you know how people are. Some folks hide it so well, it's like a second skin."

That stuck with me. Mara had always been the kind of person who lit up a room, who put others at ease. The idea that she was slowly unravelling right in front of people who didn't even notice, it chilled me. But maybe that was the point. Maybe she didn't want to be seen.

I filled Jack in on everything from my end, my meetings with Crystal, the trap we were setting, and what Reid's sister had told me. I laid out my theory, piece by piece, trying to make sense of a story that still didn't quite fit together.

When I finished, I looked over at him.

"What's your gut telling you?" I asked.

He kept his eyes on the road, silent for a moment as the wipers swept away the rain.

"I'm not sure," he said finally. "But if I had to guess... it's telling me maybe this is exactly what it looks like. A suicide. With some collateral damage."

I watched his face as he spoke, measured, uncertain, but honest.

"Maybe that's what Mara wanted," he continued. "To go out in a way that would make people look at Reid differently. Make this town that adores him finally see him for what he really is."

I let that settle in the space between us, the weight of it pressing against the fogged windows. If that was true, it was a brutal kind of justice, quiet, calculated, and devastating.

But something still didn't sit right with me.

"I can see that," I said quietly. "But it still doesn't explain the inconsistencies. If this was just about making Reid look bad, why the secrecy? Why hide the therapy? Why lie to everyone about how things were really going?"

Jack sighed, leaning back against the headrest. "People wear masks. Mara wore hers well. Maybe even better than Reid."

"Still," I muttered, shaking my head. "There's a difference between hiding pain and being deliberately misleading. The van setup, the timing, the way she pulled away from everyone, those things feel... calculated."

Jack gave me a side glance. "You think someone helped her? Or pushed her?"

"I don't know yet. But I can't shake the feeling that there's something, or someone, we're not seeing clearly. Something beneath the surface."

"You're talking about motive," he said.

"Exactly. If this was a staged suicide, what was the endgame? Revenge? Escape? Or was it a cry for help that came too late?"

Jack was quiet for a moment. Then he said, "There's something about Reid that bugs me. Every time I talk to him, he's too calm. Too… contained. Not the kind of broken you'd expect from someone who found his wife dead in the garage."

"Yeah," I said. "Grief is messy, Reid's is… rehearsed."

Jack nodded, "He's playing a role. The devoted husband, the tragic victim. But even the best actors slip eventually."

I stared out the window, the rain thickening as we turned down a narrow road. "That's why we need Crystal, and Mara's sister. They're the keys to unlocking who Mara really was in those final days, and what she wanted people to believe."

Jack looked over at me, his voice low. "You think we're close?"

I nodded slowly. "I think we're standing right on the edge of it. But one wrong step… and the whole thing falls apart."

We walked into a small waiting room, just a couple chairs, a side table with a few old magazines, and a sign that politely asked us to have a seat, the therapist was with a client. The kind of quiet that made even soft footsteps sound intrusive.

Jack and I sat, barely speaking. If we said anything at all, it was just a murmur. We both defaulted to our phones, scrolling without seeing, killing time. I rubbed my eyes, god, I wished I could take a nap, just five minutes of real sleep.

Somewhere behind the interior door, I heard the faint sound of another opening. Then footsteps, heels soft against tile. The waiting room door cracked open, and she stepped through.

She was taller than I expected, maybe 6'2", mid-thirties, with long blonde hair pulled loosely back. No-nonsense professional but without the stiffness. She had a calm energy, the kind that made you want to exhale a little slower. Her voice was soft but clear.

"Hi, I'm Dr. Ellison. Thanks for waiting, please, come in."

We followed her into a small but neatly arranged office. Her desk sat off to one side, tidy, practical. The opposite end of the room was more relaxed. A couch in a warm beige fabric, a few overstuffed chairs in earthy tones, a small table with tissues, notepads, a quiet clock ticking in the background. A diffuser gave the room a subtle lavender scent, comforting, maybe intentionally so.

"Make yourselves comfortable," she said, gesturing toward the seating area. "Would you like water or tea?"

We both shook our heads.

She took the chair opposite us, crossing one leg over the other and folding a notepad onto her lap. "I understand you have some questions about Mara."

Jack and I glanced at each other. I leaned forward.

"Yes. We're not looking to violate any privacy laws, we just want to understand where her head was. What she was dealing with. Her death... there are elements that don't line up."

Dr. Ellison nodded slowly, her expression remaining neutral. "I can't release specific details of our sessions. But I can speak in generalities, especially if I believe someone's safety was at risk or there are unanswered questions surrounding her death."

That gave me an opening. "Did she ever mention thoughts of harming herself?"

The therapist was quiet a moment, choosing her words with care. "Not directly. Mara struggled with feelings of being unseen, dismissed. She often talked about carrying other people's burdens while ignoring her own."

"Was she specific about who those people were?" Jack asked.

"She mentioned her husband, work, some old friendships. A lot of her stress seemed internal, expectations, perfectionism. She was holding everything together but felt it could all unravel at any moment."

I leaned forward slightly. "Did she ever bring up her father?"

A flicker passed through the therapist's eyes. "Yes. More recently. She'd avoided that subject for a long time, but in our last few sessions, it came up again. The manner of his death... it haunted her. She didn't say it like that, but you could feel it."

"She remembered the details?"

"She was ten, but yes, certain images stayed with her. The hose, the smell, her mother's screams. She said it came back stronger lately. Like something inside her had shifted and those memories were no longer buried."

Jack asked the next question gently. "Did she ever express anger at Reid?"

"Not overtly. But she hinted at distance between them. She described herself as invisible in her own home. There were trust issues she never unpacked fully. She'd start to talk about feeling betrayed, then pull back. A pattern I'd seen before. Like someone trying to convince themselves it wasn't a big deal."

I let that settle in.

"What about the idea of making a statement?" I asked quietly. "Of doing something that would... expose the truth? Force people to see what was really going on?"

Dr. Ellison met my gaze, calm but cautious. "She didn't say those exact words. But she talked a lot about masks. How people wear them so well that even their closest friends never see behind them. I got the sense she felt trapped behind hers."

I sat back, the pieces shifting again. If this was suicide, it was layered in intent. If it was something else... she may have seen it coming.

Jack cleared his throat. "Would you say she had given up?"

Dr. Ellison thought a long moment. "No, not given up. She was tired. But more than that, she was done pretending."

I shifted in my seat, my elbows on my knees, fingers laced.

"Can I ask you something more… general?"

Dr. Ellison nodded, resting her notepad gently on her knee. "Of course."

"Do many patients actually tell you they're seriously thinking about suicide? I mean… truly say the words?"

She looked at me, a thoughtful pause before answering. "Sometimes. But honestly? Not as often as you'd think."

I nodded slowly, then clarified, "I guess what I mean is… at the start of therapy, you have to outline the limits of confidentiality, right? That if you feel someone is at risk to themselves or others, you're required by law to report it."

"Yes, you're right," she said. "That's part of informed consent. We always explain it up front. It's the law, and ethically necessary. But," she hesitated just a second, "I like to hope it wouldn't stop someone from being honest if they're in that kind of pain. Though… in reality, I'm sure it does."

She said it gently, no judgment, just truth.

I leaned back a bit, her words settling like lead in my chest. Because I knew she was right. I'd lived it.

There was no way, back when I'd first been diagnosed with PTSD, that I would've ever admitted how close I came. How I'd sat on the edge of my bed, holding that gun in my hand, safety off, trying to find a reason not to pull the trigger. Not because I wanted to die, exactly. I just couldn't stand the weight, the hurt anymore. The silence. The chaos inside that no one else could see.

I sure as hell wasn't going to tell a therapist that, no way. Not if it meant losing control, being flagged, hospitalized, watched. The fear of being exposed outweighed the pain. So, I lied. Smiled when I had to. Talked about stress instead of despair. That was the mask I wore. The one Mara probably wore, too.

Jack glanced at me, picking up on my quiet. He didn't say anything, but I felt it. That shared understanding that comes from living with invisible scars.

I looked back at Dr. Ellison. "So, if someone was really in that space, really ready to end it… and they didn't say it out loud, would you be able to tell?"

She exhaled slowly. "Sometimes you see signs. A change in posture, language, subtle clues. But not always. Some people are very good at hiding it. Especially those who've spent their lives being the strong one. The helper. The one who's always okay."

That hit like a punch.

Yeah. That was Mara.

Once again, it felt like we were just barely scratching the surface of something deeper, something we might never fully see.

Dr. Ellison's words hung in the air long after she'd spoken to them. *Especially those who've spent their lives being the strong one. The helper. The one who's always okay.*

God, hat hit hard.

I shifted in my seat, the cushion suddenly too soft, like it was trying to swallow me whole. I glanced at Jack, who was staring down at his hands, thumbs quietly rubbing together. He hadn't moved much during the conversation, but I knew him well enough to see it, his version of flinching.

This wasn't just about Mara anymore.

It was about all of us.

About how you could wear the badge, the uniform, the smile, every layer of armour, and still be bleeding underneath. Quietly, invisibly, and how easy it was for even the most well-meaning people to look right through it.

Jack spoke up, "I remember…" he said softly. "After my first deployment. I saw a therapist, Just once. I told her I had nightmares, trouble sleeping. Left out the part where I'd wake up soaked in sweat, gasping, thinking I was back there again. I said I was tired, but not why. Never told her I'd startle every time a door slammed. That loud noises made my chest lock up like a bear trap."

Dr. Ellison didn't interrupt. She just listened. Jack kept going.

I sat there, not saying a word. I hadn't expected that from him. Maybe I wasn't the only one who'd been holding it in.

Then she asked him, gently, "You didn't say anything back then?"

Jack shook his head. "Not a word. I didn't want to get locked up. Didn't want it on my record. Didn't want anyone to know I wasn't okay."

I let out a breath—low, almost a whisper.

"Same"

Just the truth. Two grown men sitting on a beige couch in a quiet therapist's office, finally saying what we couldn't say when it might've mattered most.

Dr. Ellison nodded once, solemn but not surprised. "That's more common than you think. Especially with first responders, military, trauma survivors. You've been conditioned to be the strong one, to compartmentalize, push forward, bury pain so deep even you forget it's there."

She paused, then added, "But buried things don't disappear. They rot, they shape the way you see yourself. Then sometimes, they come back louder."

I thought of Mara then, not just the woman in the garage, or the one in Reid's carefully curated stories, but the version we were only now starting to meet. The woman behind the mask. The one who'd buried a lifetime of grief and pressure and silence beneath a polished exterior. The one who smiled for her kids, showed up to work, laughed at the right moments. Who, one day, just… stopped pretending.

Jack broke the silence. "So, if she didn't say it directly, didn't use the words, but showed you the cracks, would that have been enough to act?"

Dr. Ellison looked down at her notepad, then back up. "I monitor risk based on patterns. Language, behavior, energy shifts. But if someone is truly intent on hiding their pain, if they're motivated to not be found, it can be nearly impossible to intervene."

She leaned forward slightly, her voice softer now. "You're trying to find logic in something that lives outside of it. Suicide isn't always about wanting to die. It's about needing the pain to stop. Sometimes, the only way a person sees out is through silence. Disappearing, or leaving just enough behind to speak for them."

We sat in stillness again, the kind that only comes in the aftermath of something sacred being shared. Not dramatic, not loud. Just real. Human.

I finally stood, unsure why I moved except that I couldn't sit anymore. The lavender scent in the air was suddenly too sweet, too calming. I needed the sting of cold air, the sting of something real.

Dr. Ellison stood with us. "I'm sorry I couldn't give you more."

"You gave us plenty," I said.

She offered a small, almost sad smile. "She was complicated. But she wanted to be seen. She came here for that, even if she couldn't quite say it."

Jack extended a hand, and she shook it.

As we stepped out into the drizzle, the rain had softened into mist, the kind that clung to your jacket and hair and skin like memory. We didn't speak at first, just walked to the car, both of us replaying everything we'd heard, everything we hadn't said.

Inside the truck, I finally turned to Jack.

"I think she was screaming," I said. "Just… not with words."

He looked at me, tired and raw, and nodded.

"Yeah," he said. "Nobody heard her until it was too late."

Chapter Thirteen

This case is definitely taking its toll on me. I keep telling myself the reason I'm not sleeping is because there's more work to do, that if I just push through, if I keep my head down and stay productive, I'll finally earn some rest. But that's not it. Not really.

I get home and pour a drink. Tell myself it's just to unwind, just something to smooth the edges. But I'm so damn drained, I shouldn't need anything to help me sleep, yet, I do. Because the moment my head hits the pillow, my brain won't stop. It revs like an engine, grinding through every detail, every missed signal, every subtle look I might've misread. It's like my mind is afraid of silence, like it knows the quiet is where the truth waits.

Underneath all that noise, the hurt is creeping back in.

This time, I know what it is. That familiar ache behind my ribs, the kind that makes your chest feel tight even when you're just breathing. It's not new. I've felt it before, in other forms, with other names. It's the same goddamn shadow that's been trailing me for years. But now, I know how to bury it better. I know how to dress it up as responsibility, as focus, as drive. I know how to make it look like I've got it all under control.

But I don't, I'm tired. Not just physically, bone deep. Soul tired.

The pain's always there, pressing in from all angles. Twenty-four hours a day. The strange thing is... the case? The grind? It actually helps. Staying busy gives the pain less room to stretch out, less oxygen. If the tempo dropped, even a little, I know what would happen. I'd spiral. I'd start thinking too much, and when that happens, things get dangerous. I know what that edge looks like, and I've danced too close to it before.

So, I lie to myself. I say it's the case. The deadlines. The pressure. I say this pain is different, manageable. But I'm not fooling anyone. Not even myself. It's the same storm, just in a different season. I feel it getting closer again, like thunder rolling in behind my ribs.

I keep obsessing over her last moments, trying to get inside her head. To understand what she was thinking when she made that final choice. It's eating me alive. How does someone take that irreversible step? Especially the way she did. Carbon monoxide poisoning from car exhaust, it's not like flipping a switch. It takes time. You have to sit there, wait, breathe it in. You have to know exactly what's happening, minute by minute, as your body starts to shut down.

How do you not back out?

How do you not throw open the door and gasp for air?

It makes no sense to me. None of it does.

Then I think about a suicide I responded to years ago. An elderly woman. She walked deep into the woods, found a log to sit on, and calmly placed a plastic bag over her head. No sedation. No ties. Just sat there and held it until she lost consciousness and died.

No one forced her. No evidence of a second person. She left a note, and a few neighbors remembered seeing her strolling into the trees like she was headed for a walk in the park. It was clean, quiet, unquestionable. And still, it wrecked me.

I stood over her body that day, and all I could think was: how the hell did she do it? Every instinct we have screams for oxygen. The moment you start to suffocate, your body should panic. Should fight. Should tear that bag off your face. But she didn't. She just... let go. Like she'd made peace with it.

That case haunted me then. It haunts me now. Not because I thought it was murder, it wasn't, but because I couldn't comprehend the stillness it must've taken to let yourself drift into nothing. The kind of inner silence you need to die that way. It's something I can't grasp... and maybe that's what scares me most.

Now with Mara, I'm feeling that same cold knot in my gut. Not just the loss, but the how of it. The method. The mindset. What kind of pain makes someone override that raw, biological need to survive? What kind of ghosts were screaming in her head, and why couldn't she tell anyone they were getting louder?

Was she calm? Did she cry? Did she sit there and wait, or did she pace, second-guessing every second until it was too late?

I need to know. I have to understand it. Because if I can't figure it out, if I can't find the thread between her and that moment, then all I'm left with is the image of her in that car, alone, and the sick feeling that maybe none of us saw it coming because we were too busy, too blind, or too wrapped up in our own mess to really look.

I keep doing this, letting old cases take up permanent space in my head. I tell myself it's part of the job, part of staying sharp. But deep down, I know it's more than that. These cases live in me because some part of me wants them to. Some broken part that thinks if I hold onto them long enough, I'll eventually make sense of them, or maybe punish myself enough to feel like I've paid for not preventing them.

I know Mara had her demons too. EMS, retirement homework, she saw death regularly. She knew what it looked like when it was messy. She saw what it did to families. Maybe that made her numb to it, or maybe it gave her too clear a picture of how peaceful it could seem, in contrast to everything else. Maybe the familiarity made it feel like an old friend instead of a monster.

Here I am, staring into the same abyss again. Only this time, I don't know if I'm staring at her ghost, or my own.

But I can't ask those questions out loud. Not to Reid. Not to Sue. Not to the guys at the station. Because if I start asking them, if I let that door swing open, I don't know what I'll find on the other side.

I'm not sure I want to know.

So, I bury it, like I always do. I put on the uniform. I crack the jokes. I lift the stretcher and run the call and smile at the neighbor who waves when I get home. I keep moving. Because stopping... stopping would mean *feeling*. I'm terrified I won't be able to start again if I do.

There are nights I lie in bed, staring at the ceiling, and I wonder how many ghosts too many are to carry. I wonder if there's a number, an invisible line where the grief finally tips from manageable to fatal. Like a fire that finds oxygen and explodes.

I think I'm getting close.

But even now, I don't name it. Not as trauma, not as PTSD. I call it stress, fatigue. I tell Sue I'm just tired, that work's been heavy, that I just need to "shake this case off." But deep down, I know better. I've *known* better, I've seen it in others, I've helped talk friends through it and yet somehow, I've convinced myself I'm the exception.

That it'll pass.

That I'm fine.

I'm not fine.

I'm drowning in slow motion, and the scariest part is, I've gotten used to it.

Chapter Fourteen

The County Attorney came in right on time, sharp suit, sharper expression. We all exchanged the usual pleasantries: professional, familiar, but tight. We'd worked with him before on plenty of cases. He wasn't here to be the enemy, but he was here for answers.

He got straight to it.

"Listen, guys. I know you're working hard, and fairly. I trust you," he said, settling into the seat across from us. "But I'm getting calls. People are asking questions, people with loud voices and long memories. I need something solid I can give them. I need to be able to say: Here's what we know, here's where it stands."

He paused to let that land. His voice was calm, but the pressure was unmistakable.

"We don't want the press twisting this into something it's not. Time is of the essence. So, where are we? How fast can we close this up?"

The room went still for a beat. One of those pauses where the air feels heavy and no one wants to be the first to speak. I glanced at Jack. He gave a short nod. I leaned forward.

"We've got concerns," I said, tapping the case file in front of me. "Officially, it's still classified as a suicide. But there are enough red flags to keep us from signing off. Too many inconsistencies. Too many things that just don't sit right."

The County Attorney leaned in, elbows on the table, fingers laced together. Listening carefully.

I started from the top. "The method, carbon monoxide poisoning via vehicle exhaust. Technically possible, but statistically rare these days. Especially for a woman. Especially someone like Mara. She was strong, practical, had medical training. She'd seen death up close, EMS, long-term care, the works. This wasn't some impulsive move. It's deliberate, and that alone raises questions."

"She left no note?" he asked.

"Nothing," I said. "No note, no final message, no trail of suicidal thoughts. No digital evidence of planning or despair. Everyone we've talked to describes her as stable, not joyful, maybe even emotionally distant, but grounded. Functional. Not someone on the edge."

Jack leaned forward. "Then there's Reid."

The County Attorney gave a knowing nod. "The husband."

Jack picked it up from there. "We've been looking into Reid's behavior in the weeks before Mara's death. He'd been spending time with a woman named Crystal. Worked with him at the elementary school. We've spoken with her a couple times already. They were definitely having an affair, including having sex the night before Mara died."

"Yeah," I said. "From the moment we arrived, he was calling it suicide. Emphasizing it. Like he was trying to plant that idea in our heads. His story hasn't changed drastically, but small details keep shifting. Timeline inconsistencies, this raises red flags."

The County Attorney narrowed his eyes. "What kind of timeline issues?"

I flipped open the file again. "When we interviewed Reid the following day, he said he left his part-time job at the PD around midnight and got home 10 to 15 minutes later. Mara was awake and had been drinking. He recalled the front door sometimes didn't close properly, and that night he hadn't checked it, so he ran back to the PD to make sure it was locked. Mara tried to get him to stay, saying she wanted to go in the van and have sex like they were kids. When he insisted on going upstairs to check on the boys, she accused him of cheating."

Reid said he then went back to the PD, checked the door, and returned home. After that, he agreed they went to the van and had sex, then he went upstairs to check on the boys. He said he woke up with the sun still in his son's room, which had happened before, but usually Mara would wake him.

"The problem is," I said, "our phone records and Crystal's statement contradict this timeline, Crystal says Reid went to her house, had sex, and returned home about an hour later. That blows a huge hole in his account."

"Did the body show signs of sex?" he asked

I don't think that was looked at, at the time we didn't have reason to check for that.

"Do we exhume the body?

Chief weighed in, "Now that's a spectacle the press will eat up?

"OK good point but it's an option if that's all we have."

"No sign of forced entry?" the attorney asked. "No struggle?"

"Nothing obvious."

The County Attorney raised his eyebrows. "So, we're talking motive rooted in infidelity?"

"It's our strongest working theory," I said. "Crystal has been cooperative so far. She admits the affair, including the timing. We've asked her not to contact Reid and she's agreed, for now."

"But we don't know how long that'll last," Jack added. "Right now, it's a matter of trust. She's not under threat of charges. If her loyalty shifts, we lose that line of insight."

I leaned forward again. "Here's what I'm thinking. We can't prove what happened inside that house the night Mara died. But Reid might let something slip if he thinks he's confiding in someone safe. A few days ago, I asked Crystal to keep answering his texts. Stay engaged, but don't meet up. Just let him talk."

The County Attorney considered that. "So, she's feeding you what he's saying?"

"I have access to the texts. But if things get complicated emotionally, she might start protecting him instead of helping us."

He nodded slowly. "Alright. What about a wire?"

I hesitated. "I don't think we have probable cause, yet. I'm concerned that if word gets out, this whole thing blows wide open."

"Nonsense," he said flatly. "You've got more than enough to justify a wire under cooperative consent. Let's not waste time. I'll assign a deputy from our office to help you get it done. They'll be here this afternoon," he said, pulling out his phone and starting to text. He turned to the Chief. "Okay, Chief?"

The Chief nodded, clearly relieved to see forward momentum.

"Good, they just confirmed, they will be here in about 2 hours" the County Attorney said, standing. "Let's get this moving. The sooner we nail this down; the sooner we can quiet the noise. If there's foul play, we'll support whatever direction you take. If there's not, we shut it down clean. No circus." "Let's get the wire and then pull him in for an interview, keep me informed before that"

"Understood," I said.

He sighed, then added with a bit more weight, "I trust you both. You've handled tough cases. But I need facts, not hunches. No more smoke. Give me fire or walk away."

"We're close," I said. "There's something here. Mara wasn't reckless. She was smart. Respected. This doesn't feel like a woman who gave up. The deeper we look, the more the edges don't match the center."

The County Attorney gave a slow nod. "Get me a formal update by the end of the week. Timeline, interviews, transcripts from Crystal, anything you've got. If this turns criminal, we'll bring in the state. Be ready."

The meeting ended not long after. But the pressure didn't leave with him, it hung in the air, heavy and humming. We packed up slowly, quiet.

Every step deeper into this case was making the picture murkier, not clearer. Mara was gone, but how and why were still tangled in shadow. The one person who should have been helping us find those answers looked more and more like the one hiding them.

He left, and the door clicked shut behind him. I sat back and rubbed my temples. It felt like we were climbing a ladder with no top in sight.

Jack broke the silence. "Think Crystal's solid?"

"Solid enough for now. But I hate relying on her. She's vulnerable, and Reid's is very observant. If he smells the setup, he'll shut her out."

"She still texting him?"

I unlocked my phone and scrolled through the thread Crystal had forwarded. A message from Reid, timestamped an hour ago:

Reid: "I keep thinking about that night. You were the only real thing I had. Mara was so far gone. You were the light. I miss you."

"She hasn't replied yet," I said.

Jack leaned over and read the message. "That's not grief. That's rewriting the story."

I nodded slowly. "It's control. He's reshaping the past before the body's even cold."

We sat in silence. Jack picked at a donut; the glaze stuck to his fingers.

When I finally left the station, the sun was gone. Streetlights flickered on, casting yellow halos over wet pavement. I didn't go home right away. I drove aimlessly for a while, ending up in the old parking lot behind the elementary school, Reid's school.

I sat there, engine off, watching the silhouette of the building through the windshield. So ordinary. So quiet. Yet it felt like the epicenter of something rotten.

I thought about the staff working late, janitors finishing their shifts, teachers grading papers. I imagined Reid's office, empty now but once full of voices and energy.

After leaving the school, I found myself driving without a destination, the weight of the day pushing me deeper into my own head. For reasons I can't fully explain, maybe guilt, maybe instinct, I turned off onto the old gravel road that led to the cemetery. It was less than a mile from the station, a place I hadn't visited since the funeral. I told myself I was just passing by, just clearing my thoughts. But my hands didn't turn the wheel. They kept going.

I pulled up next to Mara's grave, shut off the cruiser, and stepped out into the heavy stillness. The air was damp and quiet, the only sound the crunch of gravel under my boots as I walked over to her headstone. I sat down beside it, leaned my back against the cool granite, and let the silence settle in around me.

I didn't speak out loud. I couldn't. It wasn't prayer, and it wasn't grief exactly, it was something in between. A quiet sort of pleading, carried only in thought. I talked to her in my head, asked her to help me understand, to guide me through the mess she left behind. To tell me what we were missing.

"What the hell happened, Mara?" I thought. "Why does none of it make sense?"

I remembered her laugh, the way she could cut through tension with a single joke, the way she always seemed to know what someone needed before they asked. She wasn't perfect, but she was sharp. She was strong. The idea that she'd just given up, alone in a van, didn't fit. Not with the woman I knew. Not with the woman everyone keeps describing.

I rested my hand on the edge of the stone, traced the lettering with my fingers. Her name. Her dates. That final dash that summed up an entire life in a single line. It made me furious. That dash didn't tell us anything. It didn't explain why a mother of two would leave her kids behind. Why someone so rooted, so present, would vanish into silence without a trace of a plan or a goodbye.

"You need to help me," I thought. "Because I can't fix this unless I know the truth, I don't think Reid's telling it."

I sat there until my legs were stiff and the wind picked up just enough to raise goosebumps. Part of me expected something, a sign, a feeling, anything. But the truth is, all I got was the cold. The absence, and maybe that was its own kind of answer.

Eventually, I stood, dusted off my pants, and looked down at the stone one more time.

"Whatever this is," I thought, "it's not over. Not yet."

I hated not knowing. Maybe we never would. But something deep inside told me we were about to find out more than we bargained for.

Chapter Fifteen

It was crowded in our small police department that morning, two deputy county attorneys, Jack, The Chief, me, and our regular patrol guy all packed into the cramped space. Crystal sat nervously in the conference room; wires being carefully attached to her by the tech team. She barely looked up as they clipped the first wire onto her purse, then another discreetly secured beneath her jacket against her body. The room hummed with tension, but since it was a public meeting, no one was too worried about Reid hugging or even touching her. That was part of the setup, to keep things natural, believable.

Outside, all our vehicles were tucked out behind the station, hidden from view. The last thing we needed was Reid spotting the observation van or any sign that we were watching. We'd borrowed a nondescript van from a couple of counties away and parked it across the street in the Hunting and Fishing store lot. It blended right in among the other vehicles, just another piece of the town's everyday backdrop. Reid had no reason to suspect it belonged to us.

I planned to be in the woods nearby, within running range if anything went wrong. Dressed head to toe in camo, I'd stay well out of sight, my only connection a small radio tucked in my pocket. It wasn't a perfect vantage point, but close enough to intervene if needed without tipping him off that we were watching. But I wouldn't know what is being said, so I was anxious because I want to know and I want to know if it's going south, I could move in, but I will rely on the observation van.

The day had started with rain, drizzling hard enough to make us worry about the visibility and the wet interfering with the wires. But now, the sun had broken through, painting the parking lot and the surrounding trees with a soft golden light. The warmth was a pleasant surprise for a fall day, just enough to make a jacket comfortable without overheating. It was perfect for Crystal, who'd chosen a jacket that could easily conceal the wire beneath it, keeping the surveillance as discreet as possible.

As I watched through the window, Crystal shifted nervously in her seat. The tension in the room was palpable, but there was no turning back now. Every second mattered. We were still plenty early, and I needed to move out soon to be in position, a good hour before the meet.

The plan was simple: patrol would drop me off at a spot we'd already scouted, tucked deep enough into the woods that no one would see me unless they were deliberately looking. The bonus? Hunting season was over. No chance of someone stumbling across me with a rifle slung over their shoulder.

We got moving. I turned to Crystal before stepping out. "Good luck. I've got your back," I said, my hand on her shoulder. "Just be natural. It's all going to be okay."

She gave a faint nod, more a reflex than a sign of confidence.

I made it into the woods without issue, careful not to leave a trail. I had my fold-out hunting chair slung over my shoulder, light, collapsible, perfect for a long sit. I found the exact spot we'd marked. Good sightlines. Cover. Isolation. I set up quickly, quiet as a whisper, and settled in.

I sent Jack a text:
In position. All clear.
His reply came fast:
Crystal's getting briefed now. Legal's walking her through it.

I could picture it clearly, the way those pre-meet coaching sessions usually went. I'd heard the same words dozens of times in undercover prep.
"Don't force anything."
"Don't beg him to confess."
"Be the shoulder to lean on but lead him gently."
"Let him talk. Act like you're just trying to understand what happened. Say you're sick over it, say it's because he came to see you that night. Let it grow from there."

Manipulation disguised as care. A mirror of what Reid had already been doing to her, but this time, she'd be the one steering it.

Still, there was no denying the risk. Crystal wasn't a cop. She wasn't trained. Whatever resentment she held toward Reid was braided with years of attraction and emotional dependency. She might crack under the weight. Or worse, get emotionally pulled back in.

But we had to try. Because if Reid was going to say something unguarded, something damning, it wasn't going to happen under fluorescent lights in an interrogation room.

It would happen here. The air was unusually still, the kind of calm that made your skin crawl if you were paying attention. Everything in this town had a sheen of normalcy, like a postcard that never changed. But today it was a backdrop for something far from ordinary. I sat half-sunk into the earth beneath a thicket of pine, the faint scent of sap mixing with dirt and old leaves. The bench was about forty yards out, near the water's edge, clearly visible from my angle. The sun threw long shadows across the clearing.

As I sat, a woman appeared, early thirties maybe, jogging stroller in one hand and a small child's hand in the other. Maybe a mother, or a babysitter. Hard to tell. They were carrying takeout bags from McDonald's. The red and yellow clashed hard against the subdued earth tones of the park. They settled on the bench. That bench. The one we needed.

They sat enjoying their fries and the filtered sunlight. Ten minutes passed. Then fifteen. We were roughly twenty minutes out from the time we needed Crystal seated, calm, casual, bait.

Jack texted. "She's on the way. Driving herself. She will park at the dirt pull-off closest to the bench."

I glanced toward the pull-off. Nothing yet. I texted Jack about the woman and child. "I'll tell Crystal to hold in her car till they move on."

I nodded even though he couldn't see me. My stomach was tight. I watched the scene, child dangling ketchup-coated fries, the woman reading a book aloud. Her voice was low, unintelligible from this distance, but the cadence was unmistakable: a bedtime story in broad daylight.

Then Crystal pulled in. Her car, a silver sedan, appeared behind the thick brush near the pull-off. Not visible from the bench, but unfortunately not visible to me either. That wasn't the plan. She was supposed to be seated, in view, wired and ready. But we weren't going to spook the family.

I stayed put.

The time came and went. Still, Crystal remained in the car. Still, the family on the bench. Still, Reid not here. My jaw tensed.

Another text came in, from our radar car near Reid's house. "He just pulled out. Running a few late."

That caught my attention. He was late. Reid wasn't the kind of guy to be late when Crystal was involved. He should've been here five, maybe seven minutes ago. What held him up?

Ten more minutes passed. Still no Reid. Still no movement from the bench. The woman had now reclined slightly, stretching her legs. The girl had laid her head in the woman's lap. Story time had become nap time.

I texted Jack. "If Reid shows, are we doing this in the car?"

After a pause, he replied: "Yes. They agree. In the car."

I sent back: "Tell her to shut it off. No radio."

"Done."

The air felt tighter, heavier. The trees didn't move, not even a breeze. A stillness that didn't feel natural.

Then I heard it. Tires on gravel. From the opposite direction, the dirt road that looped behind the lake. The one no one really used unless they knew it was there. Reid's truck came into view, crawling slow, too slow. He wasn't approaching from his house. He'd come the long way, the quiet way.

Why?

Was he checking for tails? Scanning the park to see if we were here? Or was it habit, just being cautious? My gut said this wasn't habit. He parked beside Crystal's car. Unfortunately, he parked between her and my position, blocking my view entirely.

I needed to move. Slowly, I circled the trees, keeping low, using the brush as cover. Around the far side of a large oak, I found a partial vantage point. Not ideal, but I could make out enough.

Inside the car, I saw two figures, Crystal and Reid. He kept twisting, turning, his head like a radar dish. He was anxious. His gestures were aggressive, animated. Hands slicing through the air. He leaned toward her, then jerked back, looking around again. Something about his energy was off, like a man dancing too close to a live wire.

Then, suddenly, he jumped out of her car.

He stood in the open window, leaned in, still talking, still gesturing, scanning. Then he moved quickly, back into his truck, slamming the door.

Just like that, he drove away.

The entire encounter, maybe three minutes. Maybe less, not enough. Definitely not enough.

We didn't react, we couldn't.

Crystal sat still in the car for another minute. Then, per the plan, she left. She drove east, toward the next town over, directly to the supermarket. Broad daylight. Cameras. Witnesses. In case he followed.

We waited.

Fifteen minutes later, one of our guys emerged from the hunting store nearby, got into Crystal's car, and drove off. Not toward the police station. Not yet. He headed toward the county building, thirty miles out. Just in case.

I still hadn't moved. Not until, I was sure.

Another forty-five minutes passed before I was picked up. Cruiser rolled up the dirt road, slow. We drove the entire length, twice. Eyes scanning trees, fields, mirrors. We didn't talk. My mouth was dry.

When we finally pulled away from the park, I leaned back in the seat and let out a breath I hadn't realized I'd been holding for hours.

My thoughts were racing.

What the hell just happened?

That wasn't a casual meet. That wasn't a grieving husband looking for comfort. That was someone panicked, watching, calculating. Reid's body language screamed guilt. The twisting, the frantic scanning, the energy like a caged animal trying to act like a house cat.

The way he entered the park…

Why take the back road unless you're checking for a trap?

Unless you know someone might be watching?

Unless you have something to hide?

The air in the cruiser felt tight. I rolled the window halfway, hoping for relief. There wasn't any.

My phone buzzed. Jack.

"She's wired, but it was too short. Mostly him talking about the past. Nothing actionable. We'll review it at the county building."

I nodded. It was something. But it wasn't what we needed.

Another thought hit me. What if he never intended to really meet? What if this was a test? To see who showed up? Where she parked? Whether he was followed?

If so, he played us, or tried to.

If this was a test, we needed to assume we failed.

I looked out the window, watched the trees blur into green and gold shadows.

The illusion of safety had cracked. What came next wouldn't be a conversation in a park. It would be something far more dangerous.

My gut told me this wasn't over. Not by a long shot.

The car rolled on. Ahead, a storm was coming, one we couldn't outdrive.

The meeting was supposed to give us a break in the case, a direction, a confession. But now it felt more like we'd woken a sleeping animal. I thought about the way Reid's eyes darted in every direction, his jittery hands, his explosive movements. It was more than nerves, it was strategy. He was looking for something. Or someone.

We'd prepped Crystal the best we could. The attorneys had gone over every possible scenario. They told her not to push, not to accuse, not to confront. Her job was to listen, show compassion, let him fill the silence with his own guilt. But he hadn't given her that chance. He was too busy trying to smell the trap.

The drive to the county building was long and mostly silent. I ran every second of the meet through my mind again and again. I tried to find meaning in his smallest gestures, how he moved, when he looked away, the timing of his arrival. It all felt rehearsed. Or like someone who had rehearsed his story so often, it started to crack at the seams.

In the rearview mirror, I caught a glimpse of myself, haggard, eyes heavy. This case was aging me by the hour. Every clue that emerged only led to more questions. Every step forward felt like it landed us deeper in shadow.

I thought about Mara. About her last hours. Her final conversations. Her body on the floor, and the strange serenity that surrounded it all. It didn't make sense then. It didn't make sense now.

At the county building, we met in the briefing room. Jack had already cued up the audio. We listened in silence. The room was thick with tension.

Reid's voice came through the speakers, strained, unsure. He talked about the past, their shared history, his pain. But there was no slip-up. No confession. No real explanation.

Then there was a moment, a pause in his speech, a catch in his breath. He said: "I didn't mean for any of this... I just wanted peace. I thought it would stop."

I sat up straighter.

"What would stop?" one of the attorneys whispered.

It was vague. Too vague. Not enough to charge, but enough to keep chasing. Enough to know there was more.

I turned to Jack. "We need to bring her in again. Another meet. Somewhere new. Somewhere more controlled."

He nodded, though his face looked weary.

This wasn't over. Not even close.

Next time, we wouldn't be waiting in the trees. Next time, we'd be ready to move.

Because this time, I was sure, Reid was hiding something. The cracks were beginning to show.

What Crystal saw in that moment, what she felt, would matter. It always did, witness memory isn't just about words. It's about energy, vibe, what wasn't said. There was a lot he didn't say.

In those three minutes, Reid gave away more than he realized. Not in statements, in tension, in preparation, in route. He was afraid and people who are afraid make mistakes.

All we needed now was to be there when he made the next one.

This time, we'd have more than shadows to show for it.

If that meant baiting him again, so be it. But next time, I'd be closer. No more distance. No more passive observation. If he was going to crack, I wanted to be the one watching when it happened.

Because if he really did do it, if Mara's death wasn't a suicide, then this wasn't just about justice.

It was about stopping someone who thought he could manipulate grief like a puppet on strings.

He wasn't just hiding something.

He was rehearsing.

Preparing.

Next time, we'd be the ones writing the script.

Chapter Sixteen

Well, at this point the team is split. We have a couple attorneys who don't think it's worth what we're putting into it. Me and Jack,? we think it needs more digging. The Chief is torn, he's tired. Like the rest of us, wants this whole thing wrapped up. Wants it out of his inbox, out of his mind, off the radar.

The attorneys' argument is that all we have is speculation. Circumstantial timing, a strained marriage, and a vague conversation in a car. No smoking gun. No direct link. They think Reid's little performance in the park was less about covering a murder and more about shielding his affair from the spotlight. Embarrassment over guilt. A messy man trying to manage a messier secret.

They point to Mara's history. Her father's suicide. Same method. Same silence. No note. They say that detail speaks louder than all our suspicion combined. That some patterns are inherited, some traumas echoed. That we're chasing shadows in grief, trying to assign motive to something that may simply be heartbreak.

I've thought about that a lot.

But I keep coming back to the look in Reid's eyes. The paranoia. The calculation. The back road entrance. The abrupt exit. If that was just guilt over cheating, he's the most nervous adulterer I've ever seen, and I've seen a few.

Then there's Mara. She wasn't dumb. She knew something was going on. And yeah, maybe she didn't want to frame Reid. Maybe she wasn't setting him up for a fall. Maybe she just wanted people to see who he really was. Maybe her final act was the loudest thing she ever said.

That's the part that eats at me.

There was something purposeful in the way she left things. The timing. The scene. Her positioning. It didn't scream revenge, but it whispered a kind of controlled defiance. Not a woman lost in despair, but a woman making sure her silence told a story. One that left a trail.

Jack agrees. He said, "If she was trying to disappear quietly, she would've done it differently. There was intention here. Message wrapped in method."

But the attorneys, they see grief as chaos. They say the scene felt staged because grief is messy and memory is unreliable. They don't want to chase a maybe and part of me gets that.

Except this doesn't feel like a maybe. This feels like a puzzle we haven't fully unlocked yet.

I told the Chief all this. I laid it out plainly. "We back off now, and if we're wrong, we don't get a second shot. If there's something more here and we close the book, it stays closed."

He didn't answer right away. Just looked at the window. Quiet. Tired.

Then he said, "You and Jack get one more week. Quiet. No noise. No headlines. If nothing surfaces, we're done."

A week.

That was all the air left in this investigation.

So now the clock is ticking.

Seven days to find something real.

Seven days to prove that sometimes, when you scratch beneath the surface of a tragedy, what you find isn't grief.

It's guilt.

I didn't tell anyone I was heading to Crystal's place first, not even Jack. We'd agreed it was time to press Reid, but I needed one last check. If Crystal had tipped him off about her cooperation, the entire interview could spin off course before we ever asked the first question.

Her house was quiet when I arrived, a modest two-story walk-up on the edge of town. Shades pulled halfway, a hanging plant still clinging to spring. She answered the door looking more worn than usual, like sleep had become a luxury she couldn't afford.

"Hey," she said, stepping aside.

"Hey. Just need a few minutes."

She nodded, motioning to the couch. "Coffee?"

I declined.

She sat across from me, eyes searching mine. "Is it happening? The next step?"

I leaned forward. "We're talking to him again. Soon."

Her shoulders stiffened slightly, and I noticed how carefully she folded her hands in her lap. Defensive posture. That worried me.

"Crystal," I started, "have you said anything to Reid about our last conversation? About the meeting in the park?"

She hesitated. Just for a beat, but long enough.

"No," she said. "Not directly."

"What does that mean?"

She exhaled. "He called me. Day after the park. Said he didn't think we should talk anymore. That things were getting... complicated. I asked if he meant between us or the investigation. He said both."

That wasn't nothing.

"You didn't tell him you were wired?"

"No. But I think he suspects. He said he felt like he was being tested. Like someone was watching him."

He was right, that meant Crystal had to be careful now, more than ever.

"You told the truth, right?" I asked.

Her eyes met mine, steady. "About what happened between us? Yeah. I didn't sugarcoat it."

"What about the night Mara died?"

"I told you everything. What I knew. What he said. I swear."

I believed her, mostly. But something about her expression, the way her voice dropped when she said "everything," kept me from fully exhaling. Maybe it was just fear. Or maybe there was still one piece she hadn't shared.

"He's still controlling the narrative, Crystal," I said. "Every time we give him space, he rewrites it. This next interview... it's not about catching him off guard. It's about seeing who he really is when he doesn't have time to rehearse."

She nodded slowly. "You think he did it."

"I think we don't know enough to stop asking."

I left her with that. Not a threat. Not even a warning. Just the truth.

By the time I got back to the station, Jack had already lined up the room, same neutral gray walls, same wooden table, same two chairs positioned just slightly too far apart to feel comfortable. It wasn't an interrogation room. But it wasn't casual either. Deliberately in-between. Just like Reid.

"He knows he's coming in?" I asked.

"Yeah. Said he'd be here at four. No lawyer."

I nodded. "Of course not."

Because as long as Reid believed he has the upper hand, he wouldn't ask for help. Not yet.

But the second we pressed the wrong bruise, the moment we veered too close to truth, he'd show his real hand. Maybe that was the moment we needed.

Jack glanced at me. "What's the play?"

I thought about it. Thought about Crystal's hesitation, the way Reid had circled the park like a man counting exits, the way he said, "I just wanted peace."

"The play," I said, "is no more rope. We don't give him space to spin his story. We hold the timeline in front of him like a mirror and ask him what doesn't make sense. If he lies, we'll know."

Jack nodded, jaw set. "If he tells the truth?"

"Then we'll know that too. One way or another."

As we sat and waited in the quiet, I started questioning out loud, half to Jack, half to myself.

"What are we missing?" I asked, eyes fixed on the scuffed edge of the table. "Have we looked at all the angles?"

Jack didn't answer right away. I wasn't really expecting him to. He knew the drill. Sometimes the silence before a storm has its own kind of ritual. Still, I kept going.

"Are we digging way too deep? Are we blinded by grief? Hell... maybe we *want* something to be there."

The words hung there, unanswered, heavier than I'd meant them to be.

I ran a hand down my face, leaned back in the chair, stared at the ceiling for a second.

"I mean, there's no smoking gun. Just bruises and half-truths and a timeline with cracks in it. But no solid proof. Nothing to stand in front of a jury with. Maybe they're right, maybe Mara's past was always going to lead here. Maybe all she wanted was for us to see who Reid really was before she left."

Jack finally spoke, his voice low and even. "Or maybe she left breadcrumbs because she *knew* no one would believe it. Maybe she did all she could without surviving it."

That one hit hard.

I sat with that for a second, letting it settle. The weight of it.

"I keep thinking about the way she looked at me that last time we talked," I said. "Like she wanted to say something but knew she couldn't. Like she was already halfway out the door."

Jack leaned forward, arms on the table. "You know what I think we're missing?"

I looked at him.

"Her voice," he said. "We've heard from everyone but her. Everyone telling us who she was, what she felt, what they think happened. But what about *her*? What's her side of the story?"

"She didn't leave a note."

"No, but maybe she left something else."

That thought jolted something in me, an ember that hadn't quite gone out. We'd poured over her texts, her call logs, her journals. But maybe we hadn't looked *through* them, maybe we were still reading everything at face value.

I stood up. Started pacing the room, the way I always did when a thread started to unravel in my head.

"Her calendar," I said slowly. "Her laptop. Her emails. We looked at them for *proof*, not for *voice*."

Jack nodded. "Let's pull them again. Read them like she's talking to us, not hiding something from us."

I paused, then looked at the clock.

But not now. Reid was on his way. And if he thought this was going to be a repeat of last time, a friendly chat under the guise of concern, he had another thing coming.

"No more games," I muttered. "Let's see if the truth finally shows up with him."

Jack's gaze was steady, "and if it doesn't?"

"Then we dig until we find it."

The door clicked in the distance.

Footsteps.

Showtime.

Chapter Seventeen

"Hey Reid."

I stood up and reached out, giving him the kind of hug you only give someone who's seen your worst days and stuck around anyway. In all this… we're still friends. No matter what the outcome is, that doesn't change. At least, that's what I told myself.

He hugged back, casual, maybe too casual. There was no stiffness, no hesitation. He walked in like it was just another shift, another debrief, another bullshit chat after a call. That comforted me more than I expected.

Reid had walked through that door a hundred times. He knew this room. Knew me. Knew Jack. Probably even knew where the damn scuff marks on the wall came from.

He sat down across from us like he belonged there, like this wasn't something heavier than any of us had carried before.

But he knew.

He had to know by now that this wasn't a friendly catch-up. He's no rookie, he's thorough, methodical. I taught him how to read the room, and he's reading this one just fine.

What he doesn't realize, what he's *never* seen, is what happens when I lead an interrogation this deep into an investigation that feels off from the start. He's seen me push others, break through lies, peel back stories until only truth's left bleeding on the table.

He just never thought it'd be *his* story.

Jack leaned back, quiet but locked in, letting me take the lead. It was an unspoken understanding, good cop, quieter cop. The kind of rhythm that works best when the subject forgets it's an interview.

Reid looked between us, his eyes catching mine for a second too long.

"I get why you called me back in," he said, tone neutral. Practiced. "I know you're still trying to make sense of all this."

Not defensive.

Not apologetic.

Just... managing the moment.

"Yeah," I said, keeping my voice even. "Still trying to line it all up. A few pieces aren't sitting right."

I gave him a slight nod. Friendly. Familiar.

"But first," I added, "I need to ask, have you talked to Crystal since we last spoke to her?"

There it was.

The first beat.

The first moment where truth, memory, and instinct would start colliding.

He blinked, just once. Not a flinch. Not guilt. But something flickered behind his eyes, a recalibration.

Here we go.

"Yes," Reid said after a pause, eyes lowering as he searched for the words. "We've talked a couple times."

"What were the conversations about?" I asked, keeping my tone neutral.

"Can I go back and clear some things up from before?" Reid asked.

I paused. Do I let him? Letting him talk gives him control, but it might also make him comfortable enough to slip. I decided to let him go. The more relaxed he is, the more likely we are to get something real. I'll press when I have to.

"The night Mara passed..." he started, already tearing up. Real tears. He fought to get the words out. "I didn't tell you the truth."

He stopped, took a few deep breaths, and began crying out right now.

"This is tough to admit."

My ears perked up. Jack sat up straighter. Is this it? Is he finally going to admit something more?

"I know you know now, but yes, I was unfaithful to Mara." He bent at the waist, elbows on his knees, arms hanging down into his lap.

"That hurts to say," he continued, crying openly now. "I didn't want to hurt her."

"Hurt who?" I asked gently, but directly.

"Mara," he said, the pain in his voice evident.

"How did you hurt Mara?" I asked.

"Being unfaithful, and she knew, I never admitted it to her, and I think that hurt her more than the cheating."

I let a moment pass.

"Okay. Let's get back to that night. What weren't you honest with us about?"

Reid nodded, eyes still glassed over. He wiped his face on his sweatshirt sleeve, a boyish, disarming gesture. He looked broken. Or like he wanted to look broken. Maybe both.

"I didn't tell you everything," he said slowly, staring at a fixed spot on the table like the answers were etched into the wood grain.

"Start at the beginning," I said.

"After I got home, I told Mara that I had to run back and check the door, and I came right back."

He took a breath.

"The truth is I made an excuse to go to Crystal's."

There it was. No more dancing around it. He finally put it on the record.

"She called earlier that day. Said she was checking in, making sure I was okay. I told her things were tense at home again. She offered to talk. Said she didn't want me to be alone."

"Did Mara know you were going there?"

He shook his head. "She accused me of cheating, I told you that so I guess she knew."

"And Crystal, did she know what was going on between you and Mara that night?"

He hesitated, then nodded. "Yeah. I told her that Mara accused me when I left, but that's all I never told her about when I got back."

"What happened when you got back?"

"Just what I told you, Mara had been drinking more but she was smiling and wanted to go have sex in the van like when we were kids, and we did."

"Then what? I know you have said before but tell me again, so I am not missing anything.

"We had sex, and as usual she wanted to finish, that's what the massage gun was for, I said I was going to check on the boys and I would see her in the bedroom"

"Next thing I knew I was waking up to the sunlight, I was in Owens bed, I had fallen asleep, it was like 3am when I went up, I was exhausted, and I have done that before, but Mara usually wakes me up, this time she didn't" He continued sobbing heavily.

"So, I went to look in the bedroom, she wasn't there, and I went downstairs, that's when I heard the van"

I paused, we sat quiet for what felt like an hour, Jack grabbed a water and some tissues for Reid.

Reid composed himself as much as he could.

"You need a few?" I offered

"No that's the worst of it I think, let's keep going, what else do you need?"

"Let's go back to when you went to. Crystals that night."

"What did you do at Crystal's?" I asked.

Reid looked up at me, finally. There was something pleading in his eyes.

"We had sex, we did, not love just sex, I don't know why, I am so weak."

"Weak?"

"Ya for a woman that pays me attention, I shouldn't crave it so, but me and Mara were like brother and sister most of the time"

"When was the next time you talked to Crystal?" I asked.

"Later that day, just by text."

"Did she tell you not to tell us?"

"No. She actually told me to tell the truth. Said it'd look worse if I didn't. But I panicked. I didn't want it to seem like I had something to hide, and I already lied to you at that point" holding his head, "I was embarrassed, I didn't want anyone to know, I was hoping it would go away"

"I know," he said. "I lied because I was ashamed. Not just about the affair. About not being there. About failing her."

I let the silence breathe again, giving him space, not out of kindness, but strategy. Let the weight of what he'd just said settle. Shame has a way of dragging more truth out when no one rushes to fill the quiet.

Jack scribbled something on his notepad. Not for show, he was actually writing. I didn't ask what yet.

Reid leaned forward again, elbows on the table, head in his hands. I could see the sweat soaking through his collar. Whether from the weight of confession or fear of what came next, I wasn't sure.

"You didn't want anyone to know," I repeated back to him. "What did you think would happen if we found out later?"

"I don't know," he said softly. "I guess I thought… if I could hold it together, if I didn't give you a reason to dig deeper, maybe you'd see it was a suicide, clearcut as it was. That I was just a husband who lost his wife."

"But you were more than that," I said, keeping my voice level. "You were a husband who cheated. Lied to her. Lied to us. That doesn't make you guilty of murder, but it means we must question everything again."

He didn't answer. Just nodded like he'd already had that conversation with himself a dozen times in the mirror.

Jack finally spoke.

"Reid… where were your clothes from that night?"

Reid blinked at the change of direction. "What?"

"Your clothes. The ones you wore to Crystal's, then back home. Where are they?"

"I think they're in the laundry. Or maybe I tossed them in the basket in the garage."

"You remember what you were wearing?"

"Yeah. Department hoodie. Jeans. I think." He rubbed his temples. "Why?"

"Just lining up timelines," I said. "Did Crystal give you anything? A drink, something to eat?"

He shook his head. "No. Nothing like that."

Jack's voice was steady, measured. "Did you shower at her place? Change clothes?"

"No." Reid frowned, confused now. "Why would I?"

"Just checking," I said.

127

Another pause.

"Reid," I said quietly. "When you found Mara in the garage… did anything look off? Anything at all?"

He hesitated. This time, it was more than searching for words.

"All I saw was Mara and the exhaust had filled the garage, that's why I moved the van out, to fresh air and I could pull her out that way so I could help her."

Was Reid still holding back?

"Reid is there anything else we need to know about that night?"

Reid looked up at me, something shifting in his expression. Maybe he realized we were past the point of no return.

"There's more, isn't there?" I asked.

He gave the smallest nod.

"When I got back from Crystal's, Mara was already acting different. Not just drunk. She was… off. Almost like she'd been crying, but she was trying to play it cool. Laughing too loud. Touchy. Flirty, but in a way that didn't feel like her."

"You think she was pretending?"

"Yeah. I do. Like she was performing. Like she was trying to prove something."

"To you?"

Reid hesitated. "Or maybe to herself."

He looked straight at me now.

"I don't know what she did after I left."

My stomach turned. Jack's jaw tensed.

"Why would she do that?" I asked.

"Because Mara hated feeling weak," Reid said. "If she thought someone had something over her... she wouldn't ask for help. She'd try to flip the script. Reclaim control."

"By suicide?"

"I know that's been driving me. Crazy, she loved her boys, I don't get why she left them."

"Had she ever attempted before?"

"No, nothing, no threats even"

"Had she talked to you about her Dads suicide?

"No, not in a long time, like back when we were first together"

"Her sister told us she has been talking about it lately"

"She did? well she does and always has leaned on her" "and like I said it's been a while now that we have been drifting"

I leaned back, processing.

Reid sat across from me, his posture collapsing in slow motion, shoulders hunched, hands trembling. He looked more like a man unravelling than one unburdening. But that didn't mean he'd told us everything. Sometimes confessions are just the start of a deeper lie.

Jack cleared his throat softly, a signal we'd developed after years of these kinds of interviews. Not a warning. Just... a nudge. Keep going. Stay sharp. There's more.

"You said Mara was off when you got back," I said. "Let's go deeper there. What did she say? How did she act?"

Reid nodded slowly, rubbing his palms against his jeans. "She was waiting for me. In the kitchen. Lights were low. She had one of those scented candles burning, you know, the kind she usually saves for special nights."

Jack scribbled that down. "Which scent?" he asked without looking up.

Reid blinked. "Uh... vanilla something. She always said it reminded her of her mom."

I raised an eyebrow. "Was that usual for her, using it that night?"

He shook his head. "No. That's what I mean. It was like she was trying to create a mood, or... I don't know, maybe relive something."

"Was she drinking?"

"Yeah. She had a couple wine coolers, I think. She seemed buzzed but not sloppy." He paused. "But the way she touched me, it wasn't casual. It was urgent. Like she needed to prove something."

"Prove what?" Jack asked.

"That she could still get to me," Reid said quietly. "Like she needed to remind herself, or me, that she mattered. That she still had power."

I felt the shift in the air. The kind of shift that happens when people stop describing events and start describing themselves without realizing it.

"You said she seemed like she'd been crying," I said. "Any idea why?"

"I thought maybe she'd found something, texts, maybe. Or maybe she'd just finally broken from all the distance between us. I don't know." His voice cracked again. "But she kissed me like she hadn't in years. Desperate. Almost sad."

Another silence.

Jack stood, paced a short circle, then leaned against the wall behind Reid. Flanking him, not aggressively, but with presence.

"After the van," I said, "after you had sex, and she used the massage gun... what else? Anything else strange?"

Reid shook his head. "She was quiet. Said she'd come up soon. I kissed her goodnight. I thought, maybe we'd turned a corner. Maybe that night meant something to her."

I let that sink in. "Did she say anything before you left the garage?"

He looked up. "Yeah. She said, 'You'll remember this night.' I thought she meant it… in a good way."

Jack stepped in. "That doesn't sound casual. You didn't think that was a strange thing to say?"

Reid hesitated. "Not until now."

I let the pause stretch out again. A silence that pressed against the walls.

"Reid," I said. "Do you think she set it up?"

He blinked rapidly. "What do you mean?"

"The garage. The van. The timing. You falling asleep. Her not waking you up like she always did."

He swallowed hard. "I don't know. God… maybe. Maybe she wanted me to wake up and find her. To suffer with it."

"Or maybe," Jack said, stepping forward, "she wanted to send a message. One only you would understand."

Reid's head dropped again, his hands on the table, fingers curled like they were holding onto something invisible.

"She wouldn't do that," he said, but it was weak, like a rehearsed line in a play where the actor no longer believed the part.

"You said she was performing," I added. "Trying to prove something. Was it to trap you? Punish you?"

"I don't know," Reid said, shaking his head, voice rising with emotion. "She loved me. Even when I didn't deserve it. But maybe… maybe she wanted me to carry it."

Another beat passed. A crack in the emotional shell widened.

"Do you think she knew you went to Crystal's that night?" I asked.

Reid looked up sharply, the color draining from his face.

"I… don't know. I didn't see any signs. But now?" His breath caught. "She might've known. She always knew things before I said them."

Jack stepped in again. "You said she was flirty. Desperate. Touchy. What if it wasn't about proving anything? What if it was goodbye?"

Reid blinked. "You think she planned it?"

"We don't know," I said carefully. "But we do know the scene was staged in a way that raised questions."

"She didn't leave a note," Reid whispered. "She would've left something. For the boys. For me."

"Unless she wanted the act to say it all," Jack added. "Unless she believed the silence would hurt more."

Reid's breathing grew uneven again. "What are you saying? That she… set me up to find her like that? That she wanted me to be the one to,"

"No one's saying that," I cut in gently. "But we're saying it's possible she wanted control over how she was seen, and over how *you* would be seen."

Reid leaned back, like the air had been knocked from him.

I gave it a moment, then asked, "Reid… when you pulled her out of the van, what did you do next?"

He stared into space. "I screamed. I tried CPR even though I knew it was too late. I was on autopilot."

"Did you move anything in the garage?"

"No. Just her. I mean… maybe I bumped some things. I don't know."

"Did you touch the ignition? The exhaust pipe?"

"No. The engine was still running. I turned it off after I backed out."

I nodded, jotting that down for later. It wasn't just what he remembered. It was what he *didn't* remember that mattered now.

I could see it on his face, the lines between guilt and grief were blurring. Maybe even for him.

Jack circled back to the table, stood behind his chair.

"Reid," I said, lowering my voice. "Why didn't you just tell us all of this from the beginning?"

He took a long breath. "Because I was scared. Not just of being blamed... but of facing who I've become. I failed her in life. And in death. That's something I don't get to fix."

Jack leaned down, voice quiet. "Now you have to help us figure out if you failed her in something even worse."

Reid looked at me again.

"I didn't kill her," he whispered. "But I don't know if I saved her either."

That, finally, felt like the first honest thing he'd said.

"Ok," I said finally, voice lower, slower. "This was a long day, for all of us."

"Thank you, Reid, we appreciate it, and this part will be over soon"

Reid stood quietly, softly thanked us, and walked out.

Jack gave a short nod, not quite looking up from his notes, just scribbling one last thought before dropping the pen with a quiet clack. His face said everything, he was fried. So was I. Whatever adrenaline we'd run on earlier was gone, replaced by a fog of emotional exhaustion and unanswered questions.

"Both of us need a break," I added, pushing my chair back.

Jack stood, stretching with a low grunt, the kind you let out when you've been holding your breath for too long. "You sure?" he asked. "Feels like we're close."

"Yeah," I said. "Too close, maybe. We need clear heads; not half-assed guesses built on a day of confessions and what-ifs."

He didn't argue. He didn't have to. We both knew the danger of chasing hunches without a full tank, physically or emotionally.

I walked him out. The hallway lights hummed softly, casting long shadows that stretched like ghosts along the walls. This building had always been neutral ground, meetings, strategy, debriefs. But today it felt like a confessional. A place where truths came out but never came easy.

At the door, I put a hand on Jack's shoulder. "Take the day tomorrow. Seriously. No reports. No research. No reading body language videos on YouTube."

He gave me a faint smirk. "You've been spying on my weekend habits?"

"I know you, Jack. You'll sit up all night dissecting Reid's eye twitches if I don't stop you."

He nodded again, slower this time. "You taking a day too?"

"Yeah," I said. "Gonna try. Take the boys to breakfast. Clear the smoke out of my head."

"You think we're getting close to something real?" he asked, lingering in the doorway.

"I think we've kicked open a locked door," I said. "But I'm not sure what room we're standing in yet."

Jack gave me one last look, something between concern and respect, and left.

I stood there for a moment longer, watching the night press against the glass, the parking lot empty except for our cars and the distant glow of the streetlights. The quiet after a day like this wasn't peaceful. It was too full of echoes.

Back in the room, the scent of coffee, sweat, and confession still hung in the air. I sat again, alone now, letting the silence settle in. Reid's words kept replaying, his tears, his guilt, his strange mix of transparency and restraint.

There was honesty in what he told us. That much I believed. But there were still cracks. Still missing pieces.

Worse, there was still motive.

The affair, the guilt, the change in Mara's behavior, none of it painted a clean picture. At best, it showed two broken people trying to survive in a marriage that had already collapsed. At worst...

At worst, it was a stage. A manipulation. A cover.

I exhaled slowly, letting my thoughts chase themselves in circles. Was Mara trying to provoke him that night? Force a reaction? Was the van some twisted stage for a performance that went too far?

Or was Reid still lying? Omitting something crucial?

I remembered the way his hands shook. The detail in his story. The little inconsistencies that could be panic, or they could be the edges of a fabrication.

But we needed to pause.

I pulled out my phone, shot a quick text to my wife.

Late night, taking tomorrow off. Let's take the boys somewhere early maybe pancakes.

She replied within seconds.

We'd love that. You, okay?

I stared at the screen for a moment. How do you answer that honestly, when your day's been spent watching a man crumble under the weight of a half-truth?

Yeah. Just tired.

A lie, but the soft kind.

I leaned back in my chair, letting my head rest against the cool wall behind me. In all this mess, I couldn't stop thinking about Mara. About the woman beneath the grief, the anger, the flirtation, the confusion. About what kind of pain made someone either take their own life, or make it look like they had.

Maybe that's what would haunt me the most. Not knowing. Or worse getting an answer and never fully trusting it.

Because the truth, once it's been bent and folded and twisted by enough people, never really snaps back into shape. It's like memory. Imperfect. Shaped by guilt, need, shame.

I closed my eyes.

I could still hear Reid's voice in my head. *"I didn't want it to seem like I had something to hide."*

But he did. He does. Maybe not murder. Maybe not malice.

But secrets.

Secrets that still left a young woman dead in a garage. Secrets that two boys would never understand. Secrets that turned friends into investigators and husbands into suspects.

I opened my eyes again. The room felt smaller now. The weight of the day, of what we still didn't know, settling like dust on every surface.

Jack was probably already home. Maybe standing in his kitchen, trying to shift gears into dad mode, pretending his brain wasn't still running red lines of dialogue and timeline checks.

I'd do the same soon.

But I knew, even as I shut off the lights, even as I locked up and stepped out into the heavy night air, that neither of us would really sleep. We'd carry this with us, let it chew on the edges of our thoughts, turn over each sentence Reid said like a puzzle piece we're trying to force into a shape that never quite fits.

Even if we get the truth, whatever that ends up being, I know this is one of those cases. The kind that stays with you.

Where no matter how much evidence you find, no matter how many interviews you conduct, no matter how many timelines you stitch together,

There's always that one corner of doubt you carry with you.

Forever.

Chapter Eighteen

Even though I haven't had a full night's sleep since all this started, I was up before the sun. Before the boys. Before Sue. I'm not even sure I slept. Just a blur between watching the ceiling fan spin and replaying Reid's voice over and over again in my head.

I padded quietly into the kitchen, the house still cloaked in that soft morning hush. There's something sacred about these few minutes, when the world hasn't quite woken up yet and your thoughts are still yours, untouched by the weight of the day.

I started the coffee. Not because I needed it, though I did, but because Sue would appreciate it when she came down. I always liked doing that. Something simple. Predictable. Normal.

The smell filled the kitchen and for a second, I could almost pretend today was just any other Sunday.

The boys would be up soon. I could already hear the faint stirrings from their rooms, closet doors sliding open, soft thuds of feet hitting the floor. They had no idea what I carried with me this week, and I was grateful for that. I needed this house to stay innocent, untouched by what I couldn't unsee.

After breakfast, I thought maybe a ride would do us all some good. North sounded nice. Somewhere past the tree line, where the air smells like pine and damp leaves and you feel like maybe the world's just a little simpler.

Sue loves the outlets up there. She could lose herself in a few shops. I'd lose myself in a mountain road, windows down, music low, just... breathing. More than anything, it wasn't *here*. I didn't have to worry about running into someone who might casually ask, *"Hey, you hear about Mara?"* and not realize how deep that rabbit hole went for me.

That's the danger in a small town, everyone thinks they know something, everyone wants to talk and when they don't get answers, they fill in the blanks. Theories, whispers, assumptions. All it takes is one sideways look at the grocery store to make you second-guess what you thought was true.

No, we needed distance today. I needed distance.

Of course, I'd still be thinking about it. That's inevitable. There's no switch to flip, no magical mental off-button. But the truth is, my bonus for the day, the real reason a long drive didn't feel like avoidance, was Sue.

She's a hell of a sounding board when I let her be. Smart, patient honest in a way that cuts through the fog, and right now, I needed that. I needed an outside perspective. Someone not tied into the web of emotions and history this case has tangled around me.

Sue's never been in law enforcement, but she knows people. Reads them well and more than once, her observations have cracked something open in my thinking that I hadn't seen coming. She has a way of asking the one question that matters. The one that makes you stop and go back and look again.

I poured a mug and sat at the kitchen table, the old wood cool beneath my hands. Sunlight was just starting to stretch through the blinds, casting angled shadows on the floor.

Reid's voice crept back in again.

"She said she didn't feel safe... but I didn't think she meant it like that."

What did she mean?

Was that fear real, or performative? Desperate or manipulative?

What about Crystal? She hadn't left my mind either. There was something off in that dynamic, like we were standing in the middle of a chessboard with pieces we hadn't even seen yet.

I took a sip and closed my eyes. I wasn't going to solve it right now. Not here. Not on three hours of broken sleep and half a cup of caffeine. But maybe, if I could just talk it out, lay it all out with someone who hadn't been in the room with Reid, someone who didn't have all the same emotional fingerprints on the scene... maybe something new would surface.

Footsteps on the stairs.

Sue.

She stepped into the kitchen wrapped in one of my old sweatshirts, hair pulled up, eyes soft with that look that somehow always said, *"I know you're not saying everything, and I'll wait until you're ready."*

"Coffee?" I offered, already standing.

"You read my mind," she said with a quiet smile.

I handed her the mug and sat back down, watching her take the first sip. The warmth of her. The steadiness. After a week full of death, suspicion, and unravelling trust, it was jarring, in the best way, to sit across from someone whose love didn't feel like a question.

"I was thinking," I said carefully, "maybe we take a drive today. Head north. You can raid the outlets, and I'll get some fresh air."

She gave me a look. Not suspicious. Just perceptive.

"You trying to clear your head or run from it?"

"Little of both," I said. "But I'd like to talk to you about something. Work stuff."

She nodded. "Then let's go."

After we had a great country breakfast, eggs, bacon, pancakes, the works, and our bellies were full, we packed into the truck and started heading north.

The world felt different as soon as we got out of town. Like we'd crossed some invisible line between the everyday noise and something quieter, something simpler. It was the kind of fall day that reminds you why you live in New England. That perfect crispness in the air, not cold enough for a coat, just right for a favorite sweater. The kind you've had for years, soft at the sleeves, broken in just right.

The leaves had hit their peak, flaming reds, bright golds, deep oranges like fire frozen in the treetops. Every gust of wind sent a swirl of them dancing across the road. They crunched under our boots when we stopped at the scenic overlook later, brittle and dry and satisfying in that way only autumn leaves can be.

The smell, God, I love that smell. The woodstoves puffing smoke from chimneys, that sharp tang of burning maple and oak. The earthy scent of fallen leaves beginning to decay, mixed with pine and dirt and something sweet in the air that always makes me think of home.

It's more than just a season, fall. It's a feeling. Like a deep breath. A reminder to slow down. To notice things.

Sue rolled the window down a little, let the cool air swirl in, and I caught her smiling to herself as we passed a field lined with pumpkins and scarecrows. She leaned her elbow on the door, her hair blowing a little in the breeze, and I could tell she needed this just as much as I did.

For a while, we didn't talk. Just let the hum of the tires and the soft rock station on the radio fill the silence. It wasn't awkward. It was the kind of quiet you can only share with someone who really knows you. Who doesn't need to fill space with words.

Eventually, she looked over at me.

"So," she said. "Work stuff?"

I kept my eyes on the road, fingers tightening slightly on the wheel. I knew she'd wait for me to open the door on it.

"Yeah," I said after a beat. "You know it," Heck our friends are the players. "I don't even know what I'm chasing anymore, truth, closure, or just trying not to drown in it."

She didn't respond right away, just let me talk, and I would, eventually. I just needed a few more miles, maybe a side road through the woods, maybe one of those long stretches where the trees make a tunnel overhead and the light flickers just right, like the whole world is giving you a moment to think.

I also couldn't outright give details, not with the boys around. They might have their headphones in, but they pick up on everything. Every word. Every shift in tone.

Sue knew that too. So, when she leaned in just slightly and asked, "How's Reid doing?" it was her quiet way of saying *I'm on the same page now.*

I kept my eyes on the road, the lines blurring under the tires. "He's… stressed. We had a long talk yesterday. It was tough. He's hurting."

She nodded slowly. No need to say more just yet.

"And the boys?" she asked.

"His parents have been staying at the house. Helping out, keeping them in a routine. It's the right call. He couldn't manage alone right now."

She didn't respond right away. I could tell she was piecing things together in her head, as she always does. A mother's lens. A wife's lens. That quiet wisdom I've leaned on more times than I can count.

"He has a new friend," I added, lowering my voice just slightly. I tried to keep it vague, but the tone was enough to signal something more. Something strange.

Her brow lifted a little. "Oh?" she said, not pressing yet. "That's odd. He usually keeps to himself. Doesn't seem like the outgoing type."

That was Sue's polite way of saying *he never struck me as someone who would step out.* She had watched Reid at cookouts, holiday gatherings, those nights when we'd invite a few couples over. He was the quiet, steady one. Family man. The kind who brings the deviled eggs and leaves early to get the kids to bed on time. No flash. No edge.

But she was taken by what I'd said. I saw it in the way she shifted in her seat, pulled the blanket over her lap tighter, and looked out the side window. She didn't ask right away. She let it sit there between us, floating in the quiet.

Then, gently, "Somebody from work?"

"Yes," I said, keeping my tone even. "Matter of fact… they do work together."

I didn't look over. I didn't have to. I could feel her expression shift just from the silence. I knew exactly the shape of it, surprise, concern, calculation. She was fitting this new piece into her mental image of Reid. It didn't sit quite right. Not yet.

"That's messy," she finally said.

I nodded. "Very."

She turned back to the window, her breath fogging the glass just a little. I could tell she was weighing whether this 'friend' was just emotional support, or something more. Something riskier. Something that made a grieving husband look a little less like the victim and a little more like the center of a story he wasn't telling all.

"You think this started before?" she asked, her voice softer now, like she didn't really want to hear the answer.

"Yes, it did," I said honestly.

Sue didn't respond right away. She leaned back in her seat, turning her face toward the window again. Her silence wasn't avoidance, it was her way of absorbing, processing, thinking. A long stretch passed where neither of us spoke, just the sound of the tires on pavement and the quiet hum of the radio. Something soft and folky played, one of those acoustic songs that always made road trips feel slower, steadier.

The fresh air drifting through the open window carried that woodsmoke and distant pine scent, grounding me. But my mind was still tangled, sorting timelines, replaying conversations, weighing body language against the truth Reid swore he told. Everything still felt just out of reach, like a puzzle with a missing middle piece.

We pulled into the small downtown strip a little after noon. It was quiet this time of year, tourist season winding down. Just a few scattered cars along the tree-lined street, a coffee shop with two people out front, and the park across from it with that wide green lawn and old wooden playground. The boys lit up when they saw it, unbuckling before we even came to a full stop.

"Go ahead," I said, nodding to them. "But stay where we can see you."

Sue and I walked slowly to a bench near the edge of the grass. We sat in the sun, the breeze tugging lightly at our sleeves, watching the boys climb and chase and laugh. I envied their freedom, how completely untethered they were from the weight of everything that had settled on my shoulders.

I took a breath, then gave her the whole thing. The talk with Reid, the red flags, the unease that kept growing. I laid it out like a case file, but with more hesitations than conclusions.

Sue was quiet but focused, she didn't interrupt, didn't push. She just listened, taking it all in with the same steady patience she always had. Then, like she always did, she started asking questions, thoughtful ones, sharp ones.

"Do you think Mara was doing it as a cry for help?" she asked, after a pause. "Figuring Reid would come back down looking within a few minutes?"

That hit me hard. I hadn't considered that angle, not really. But as soon as she said it, something shifted in my chest. The possibility made sense. It explained a lot.

It would explain the missing note. It would explain the messiness, the suddenness, the way the whole thing felt too unresolved. It could've been a desperate move, not meant to be final. A tragic miscalculation.

Then my mind snapped to the scene again, the garage, the hose, the exhaust pipe.

"No one confirmed the hose was actually in the pipe," I murmured, mostly to myself. "We all just assumed because of where it was lying. But it wasn't wedged in, not really. When I rubbed my hand along the pipe... barely any soot. No markings like it had been jammed in and sealed."

Sue turned to me, eyes narrowing. "So, you think... it might not have even been set up right?"

"I don't know," I admitted. "But if it wasn't sealed, then the whole thing gets even murkier. If she was trying to make a point, not end her life, it could explain everything. If Reid walked in and found her... maybe he panicked. Maybe he thought it was too late and staged the rest to look more definitive, or maybe,"

"Maybe he just let it happen," she said softly, finishing my thought.

I looked out across the park. The boys were throwing leaves at each other now, laughing like they hadn't a care in the world. Maybe they didn't, that's how it should be.

But for me, for Sue, for the people left holding pieces of something broken, it never stayed that simple.

Our talk did help, got it off my chest, helped me relax, Sue's help as always was awesome. The rest of the day I enjoyed walking the shops in downtown and then the outlets along the highway, me and the boys snuck off and grab an ice cream while Sue was shopping.

We pulled into home at about 8 pm, a great day, a couple meals on the road, many miles of family bonding. I finally felt exhausted, and I was able to lay down.

Chapter Nineteen

For the first time in weeks, I woke up rested, and not just physically. Something inside felt lighter. The weight that had been pressing down on my chest every morning wasn't gone, but it had shifted just enough to let me breathe again.

I got up without hesitation, threw on jeans and a hoodie, grabbed a Pop-Tart on my way out the door, and hit the road before the rest of the house stirred.

The early air was cool and crisp, the kind that makes you feel like you're ahead of the world. For once, I was ready to take it on.

When I walked into the station, Jack was already there, coffee in hand, going through paperwork with that tired-but-grounded look he carried most days.

"How was your day off? Do anything fun?" I asked, my energy high, almost annoyingly so for how early it was.

Jack smirked. "It was good. We headed over to Tuttle's Farm. Picked apples, grabbed a couple of pumpkins. The kids had a blast. Honestly… it helped. Cleared my head a little."

"Excellent," I said, genuinely happy to hear it. "We went up north. Just hung out, took in the air. Needed that reset."

There was a beat between us, the kind that settles like a mutual understanding. We both knew the case wasn't going away. We'd be stepping right back into it soon. But the break, however short, had done its job. It gave us space to step back, breathe, and recalibrate.

"I've been thinking," I added, dropping my bag on the desk, "about some things Sue said. She sees it from a different angle and honestly… it's changed how I'm looking at a few pieces."

Jack glanced over, his face sharpening slightly. "Good. I've been mulling a few things myself. Maybe it's time we lay it all out again. Fresh eyes."

"Exactly," I nodded. "Let's go back to the beginning, walk through it slow, no assumptions."

Because now, we weren't just reacting, we were ready to dig.

We moved into the conference room, that familiar neutral space where distractions felt minimal and the work got serious. I pulled the whiteboard out from the wall and grabbed a couple of markers from the tray, double-checking this time to make sure they weren't permanent. I'd made *that* mistake before, and Jack still brought it up anytime he wanted to get under my skin.

He slid a legal pad across the table, flipping to a blank page. "All right," he said. "Let's lay it out."

By the time we were ten minutes in, the board was already starting to resemble a messy Venn diagram, names, arrows, question marks, timelines all overlapping in what looked like chaos but made perfect sense to us. We took turns at the board, scribbling connections, rubbing out dead ends with our sleeves, stepping back to squint at the bigger picture.

We debated every little detail hard. Sometimes we'd loop back on the same point three, four times, trying to poke holes or see something new in the cracks.

"Okay, let's go back to the night of," Jack said, pointing at the timeline on the far left of the board. "Reid says he went up to bed around 3 am. Mara stays downstairs. We know what time the call came in. But what about everything in between?"

I circled the 07:05 AM timestamp in red. "That's the emergency call logged. Based on our timeline, there's at least a four-hour gap unaccounted for. No one saw her in that time, but she was found where he left her"

"Nobody saw Reid either," Jack added. "At least not in any verifiable way. Just his word he was upstairs asleep."

I drew a dashed line between their bedroom and the garage. "If she wanted him to find her… why the garage? Why not somewhere he'd go?"

"Unless she *didn't* want him to find her," Jack countered. "Or maybe…" He trailed off, tapping the marker against his lip. "Maybe she *did*, but she misjudged the time. What if she thought he'd come down right away?"

I stopped. "That's exactly what Sue said yesterday."

He looked at me, surprised. "Really?"

"Yeah. She said maybe it was a cry for help. A moment of emotional overload. That she might've expected Reid to come back downstairs in a few minutes and stop her."

Jack leaned back in his chair, letting that sink in. "That would explain no note. Would explain the hose just barely being in. Would explain why nothing about that scene felt fully committed."

I nodded. "Also explains the light dirt on the tailpipe. It wasn't jammed in, it was just placed. Almost like she was staging the idea of suicide rather than really trying."

Jack exhaled slowly. "Damn. So, then what? He didn't come down. Or he came down and didn't stop her?"

We were quiet for a minute. Heavy silence. Those kinds of thoughts had weight to them.

Eventually, I picked the marker back up. "Let's list everything we're missing. What we need to confirm, refute, or dig up."

Jack clicked his pen. "Okay. First: confirm who last physically saw Mara alive. Not just by phone or assumption."

"Second: Forensic confirmation on the hose. Was it handled? Wiped? Positioned? Is there trace evidence we haven't processed?"

"Third," I added, "the new friend. Crystal. Need to trace *exactly* when that relationship started. Could be motive, could be misdirection."

We kept going like that for hours, back and forth. Outline and debate. The kind of working session where time disappears and the board becomes the only thing that matters.

Somewhere in the middle of that messy web of ink and questions, something started to take shape, faint, like a silhouette in fog, but there.

It was time to make the call.

The conversation with the Chief and the County Attorney had been a long time coming, and now that we'd organized everything, there was no excuse to hold back. I picked up the phone, my fingers pausing for just a second before dialing. Within minutes, the Chief and the County Attorney agreed on a 5 p.m. meeting at station, thank god I didn't want to try to recreate that white board.

That gave Jack and me about four hours, just enough time to grab a bite, maybe decompress for a bit before what was sure to be a pivotal conversation. I locked the conference room behind us, the cluttered whiteboard still fresh in my mind even as we stepped out into the fading afternoon light.

"Go home, get something decent to eat," I said to Jack as we reached the parking lot. "We've earned a minute."

"Copy that," he said, giving me a tired smile.

When I got back later that afternoon, the air had a different weight to it. Not heavy exactly, but full. The kind of energy you get before a storm, when everything feels on edge but not yet chaotic.

The Chief was already there, seated in his office with the door cracked open. I knocked gently and stepped in. He looked up and offered a tired smile.

"Before anything else," he said, "how are you doing?"

The question caught me for a second. It wasn't about the case, or the evidence, or the media pressure that was surely around the corner, it was about me. About the toll this was taking, and the sincerity in his voice wasn't something I took lightly.

"I'm okay," I said. "Better today actually. Yesterday helped."

He nodded and motioned to the chair across from him. "Sit for a minute."

We talked. Not about the case, not yet. Just about life. Family. The kind of conversation that reminded me he wasn't just the Chief, he was someone who had walked through fires of his own. It was a welcome pause, a breath in the middle of it all.

Jack arrived not long after. The Chief greeted him the same way, asking about his kids, his day off, how he was holding up. Just like that, the three of us sat there, talking about anything *but* the case, letting the tension ease out of the room before the real work began.

Then the County Attorney arrived, flanked by two deputies who'd been instrumental in helping us piece together parts of the timeline. Their presence brought a subtle shift in the energy, more formal now, more focused.

I got up and led them down the hallway to the conference room, flipping on the lights as we entered.

They stopped short at the door.

The whiteboard.

It was still as we'd left it, covered in arrows, boxes, circles, timestamps, notes scribbled in different colors, overlapping questions and connections that looked like a conspiracy theorist's living room wall.

One of the deputies let out a short laugh and pointed. "I hope *you* can make sense of that."

The County Attorney chuckled too, eyes scanning the chaos. "It's either a brilliant investigation," he said, "or a nervous breakdown."

"Possibly both," I admitted with a grin. "But I promise, it makes more sense than it looks."

They found their seats, the energy shifting again, this time into the territory of something real, an inflection point. We had their attention now. The next few minutes would define where this case went from here.

I took a breath.

Then I began.

This time, I didn't hold back.

From the moment everyone settled into their seats, I walked them through everything, start to finish. A full, uninterrupted presentation. Jack stepped in at key points, reinforcing the facts, pointing out our shared concerns, but mostly he let me lead. We made sure to circle back to the red flags we'd mentioned the last time we met, only now we had more weight behind them. More clarity.

The room was quiet, but focused. This wasn't a courtroom, not yet, but the air had that same silent pressure. Everyone was listening, watching. I could feel their thoughts catching up to our timeline, tracking the inconsistencies, the emotional undercurrents.

Once we wrapped the narrative, the questions came, but they weren't hostile. Not even guarded. More conversational. Clarifying. It felt like we were all on the same side of the table, at least for now.

Then the County Attorney shifted forward in his seat, fingers laced together. His voice was calm, but direct.

"What do *you* think this was?"

Not *you all* as he waved his hand toward everyone. Not *what does your department think.*

Just *you.*

I looked at Jack, then at the Chief, then back at the table of attorneys. I wanted no confusion.

"This is just my take," I said. "This isn't coming from Jack. It's not from the Chief. This is me."

I paused, just for a second. Then I spoke, clearly and deliberately.

"I believe Mara was making a cry for help. I think she intended for Reid to come back down, to find her within a few minutes. I believe she thought he'd realize she was gone and come after her. But he didn't, he fell asleep, and at some point, she did too. With the alcohol in her system and the exhaust fumes building, I don't think it took long."

I could feel the words settle over the room like fog, soft, but heavy.

"This theory explains why there was no note. Why the setup wasn't as precise or planned as we'd expect. Her mindset didn't seem to reflect someone who had fully committed to ending her life. Then there's the hose, no confirmed witnesses placing it in the exhaust pipe. When I rubbed my hand over it, there was barely any soot. It wasn't convincing. It feels like a setup done quickly, maybe even in the dark."

I let the weight of it land.

"She was hurting, she knew Reid was cheating. Maybe in that moment, she thought this would shake him, scare him. Bring him back to her. I don't think she wanted to die that night, I think she wanted to save what was left of them."

I scanned the room as I finished, catching subtle nods, the flicker of understanding behind the eyes. No one interrupted. No one scoffed. There was a shift, small, but real. Agreement? Maybe. Or at least respect for the possibility.

Then I turned to Jack.

"Jack, what's your theory?"

Jack leaned forward, his hands folded on the table, eyes scanning the whiteboard as if organizing his thoughts before speaking.

"I agree with most of what he said," Jack began, nodding toward me. "But I've also been running through every scenario, every version of that night, and I keep coming back to something slightly different."

He paused, not for effect, but to make sure his words were measured.

"I think it might've started as a cry for help… but I don't think it ended that way."

That caught attention. A few heads tilted slightly. The Chief glanced at him with a raised brow but didn't interrupt.

"I think Mara *did* want to scare Reid. To shake him. Maybe even manipulate the moment emotionally. But I think once she got in that car… something shifted. Maybe it was the alcohol, maybe it was a wave of despair. I think the line between a cry for help and a real attempt blurred for her. By the time she might've wanted to stop it… it was too late."

He rubbed his temple with his thumb, tired but clear.

"I've spent a lot of time looking at her text history, tone changes in her messages, even her social media activity in the weeks leading up. She wasn't consistent. One day hopeful, the next withdrawn. That erratic swing, it makes me think she was emotionally unstable in a very dangerous way."

He looked around the room now.

"I don't believe she meticulously planned this. But I also don't believe it was completely impulsive. It's that dangerous middle ground, the kind where you don't know you're serious until it's too late."

He glanced over at me again. "I trust his instincts. I think he's right, she thought Reid would come after her. But I also think she was mentally in a place where the worst outcome didn't feel so far-fetched anymore."

The room was quiet again. A different kind of quiet this time, one filled with implications, possibilities.

Jack finished with a soft exhale.

"So, no… I don't think this was a clean-cut suicide. I don't think it was an accident. I think it was a moment of emotional chaos, and the setup was just enough to tip the balance."

The County Attorney took over, leaning back just slightly as he let the weight of everything settle over the room.

"Alright," he said, his voice calm but deliberate. "We've heard from the front-line investigators, in either theory, they're in agreement. This doesn't rise to criminal conduct."

He looked around the room, gauging the reactions. "Does anyone feel differently? Speak now."

There was a moment of silence, then one of the deputies, a younger guy, but sharp, spoke up.

"Actually, I just want to say, after hearing their breakdown and reviewing everything we've got, I'm with them. I absolutely agree with both theories. We may never be able to nail it down to one final conclusion but based on the evidence... it's not criminal."

He nodded toward us, "You guys did the work, no stone unturned, and it shows, Great job."

There was a quiet ripple of affirming murmurs around the table. A few more nods. Not celebration. Just something close to professional closure.

I felt my shoulders ease for the first time in days. Not because it all made sense, it didn't. Not because the outcome felt satisfying, it never would. But because we'd done what we could. We followed the threads to their end, even when the lines blurred.

Jack caught my eye and gave a small nod. The Chief stood up and said, "Let's write this up right, then get some rest. You've earned it."

For the first time, I believed it.

Chapter Twenty

I headed to Reid's directly from the meeting. I wanted him to be the first to know the investigation was over. No more questions. No more interviews. No more dragging him through this. I hoped it might ease his pain, give him back a sliver of peace.

But my own weight hadn't lifted. Not yet. Not fully.

Maybe it was the residue of everything. Or maybe it was something deeper, something nameless gnawing at the edge of my thoughts. I couldn't tell anymore. The difference between exhaustion and erosion had blurred. Whatever it was, it clung to me, like the smoke that sinks into your uniform after a fire. You don't notice it right away, not during the heat of it. But it follows you home, into your clothes, your pillow, your lungs and into your bones and dreams.

When I pulled into the driveway, the house looked... still. A few lights were on. His parents' car sat out front. On the surface, it looked like peace had returned, like the Hollywood version of a family trying to move forward. One of those quiet cul-de-sac homes where everyone waves and barbecues on Sundays.

But I knew better.

That house held the kind of silence you can feel. Not calm. Not restful. Just... hollow.

I stepped out of the car slower than usual. It was like gravity had tripled. Every movement a small negotiation. My boots scraped the gravel, and it sounded too loud, like I was intruding.

Reid's father opened the door. His face looked like a faded photograph, tired and fraying at the edges. But he gave me a kind nod and said, "He's out back."

I found Reid in one of those old Adirondack chairs, the kind that never quite sit level on the grass. Hoodie pulled over his head. A beer bottle cradled against his thigh like it might slip away. His eyes were fixed on nothing.

I sat next to him without a word. The night was cool. You could hear a dog barking down the street, the low hum of distant tires on asphalt, a soft creak of tree branches moving above us.

Eventually, I said, "It's over. Investigation's closed."

He nodded, not looking at me. "And?"

"And we don't believe there was criminal intent," I said. "Not from you. Not from anyone."

Another nod. Still not meeting my eyes. "So that's it then."

"Yeah," I said. "That's it."

The words hung there, useless. They didn't land like I thought they would. No relief. No exhale. Just more weight.

He took a sip. I watched his fingers tremble.

"I still think about her face," he said, voice barely above a whisper. "Every night when I close my eyes."

I didn't respond. I didn't have a response. I wasn't here to fix him. I wasn't sure I could fix anything anymore. I just wanted to bring him closure. But the truth is, closure's a myth. A story we tell ourselves so we can keep getting out of bed.

He turned to me, finally. His eyes were red-rimmed, but dry. "Can I ask you something? Off the record?"

"Of course."

"What if I had gone down that night? What if I'd opened the garage?"

I hesitated.

"Then maybe we're not sitting here," I said. "Maybe she's still alive. Maybe not. I don't know."

He nodded, slow and deliberate. "I think about that too."

I wanted to tell him the rest. About my theory. That maybe… maybe she hadn't meant to die. That maybe she was just waiting for him to save her. That maybe it wasn't a cry for help, but a test of love. I wanted to say it, but I didn't. He was already carrying enough. No sense loading the dead onto his back too.

We sat in silence, just the two of us and the ghosts we didn't name.

"Want a beer?" he asked suddenly, voice dry like old paper.

"No, brother," I said gently. "I've got to get home. Haven't seen Sue or the boys much lately, and I'm running on fumes."

"I'm sorry," he said, eyes downcast. "Guess that's my fault."

"No. No, it's not," I said quickly, sharper than I meant to. "None of this is your fault."

But he didn't believe me. I could see it in the way he stared through the grass, jaw clenched like he was trying to bite back everything he couldn't say.

"I should've told you everything from the start," he muttered.

"It's okay. I get it."

I did understand. We all hold pieces of ourselves back, sometimes for protection, sometimes out of shame. Sometimes because the truth feels like a confession that will destroy what's left.

When I finally pulled away from the house, I felt heavier than when I'd arrived. My job was done. The box had been checked. But something inside me dragged like a chain behind the bumper. Something unfinished.

I couldn't shake the feeling that I had been changed by this, irrevocably, and not in some poetic, soul-deep kind of way. I mean physically. Mentally. Like this case had punched a hole through my foundation and I just hadn't noticed the cracks forming yet.

I was angry. Furious, even. This never should've landed in my lap. We should've called in the state immediately. Let them take it cold and clean and by the book. Maybe then I wouldn't be driving home feeling like I'd just walked out of someone else's tragedy with the blood still on my hands.

As I turned onto the highway, I glanced in the rearview mirror. His porch light was still on, glowing like a lighthouse through the trees. Or a warning.

I told myself I'd leave it all behind now. Go home. Breathe. Hug my kids. Hold Sue tighter than usual. Let this thing settle into the past where it belonged.

There are some calls that never really end. They don't tie off neatly with paperwork or a closed file. They echo. Long after the scene is cold. Long after the uniforms are folded and the statement is signed.

This one had its claws in me, and not just because it was personal. Not because it was Reid, but because something about it had cracked open a door I didn't know existed in me.

Now it wouldn't close.

But in the hum of the engine and the rhythm of the tires on the road, I heard her voice again.

She was waiting for him...

I turned up the radio. Louder than it needed to be.

Didn't help.

Some stories don't end when the case closes.

Some stay with you. Some dig in.

I told myself I'd leave it all behind now. Go home. Breathe. Hug my kids. Hold Sue tighter than usual. Let this thing settle into the past where it belonged.

But the truth was, I knew it wouldn't stay there.

There are some calls that never really end. They don't tie off neatly with paperwork or a closed file. They echo. Long after the scene is cold. Long after the uniforms are folded and the statement is signed.

This one had its claws in me, not just because it was personal, not because it was Reid. But because something about it had cracked open a door I didn't know existed in me.

Now it wouldn't close.

That night, I didn't sleep.

I lay there staring at the ceiling while Sue's hand rested lightly on my chest, rising and falling with my breath like it could keep rhythm for me.

But my mind was racing, Not with questions, Not even with guilt.

Just static, cold, colorless static.

I kept thinking about Mara's eyes. Not when we found her, but from years ago. The way she looked when she laughed too hard at Jack's bad jokes. The look she gave Reid when he wasn't paying attention.

I kept thinking about Reid about the weight he carried. About the way he asked, *"What if I'd gone down there?"* and how the silence after hung heavier than the answer.

I should've felt relief, the case was closed. The burden should've lifted.

But it didn't, it shifted.

From task to memory, from duty to permanence.

Work went on, shift after shift. Calls came, we responded, fires, overdoses, wrecks, suicides. We cleaned the rigs; we drank our coffee. We cracked our dark jokes and pretended it made us whole.

But I wasn't whole.

I wasn't aggressive like I used to be, I wasn't sharp, I hesitated more. I let other guys take the lead, I caught myself zoning out during briefings, during meals, during moments that should've mattered.

I moved like a machine. I spoke on autopilot. I listened, but I didn't always hear.

The radio would chirp, and I'd respond like nothing was wrong.

But something was wrong. I just didn't know what to name it yet.

The tightness in my chest wasn't just fatigue. The cold in my bones wasn't just from the weather. The constant ache behind my eyes wasn't just bad sleep.

I didn't know I was unravelling, I didn't know I was broken.

Not then,

but looking back now, I think that's when it really started.

Not when I saw her, not when I watched Reid fall apart, not when I closed the file.

It started here, on that dark stretch of road, her voice echoing in my head, and the realization that no matter how fast I drove, I couldn't outrun it.

It started with the silence that followed,

The kind of silence that doesn't end,

Eventually, I stopped pretending I wasn't on fire.

One Sunday night, ten minutes after signing on and heading out on patrol, I was back at the station. I just couldn't do it, I was mentally spent, I had one choice.

I walked in, dropped the keys on the desk, and wrote my final sign-off like I was clocking out for a lunch break. My gear stayed behind, hat, jacket, radio, each piece of it heavy with years of memories I couldn't carry anymore.

No speeches, no drama, no goodbye party.

Just… done.

I didn't linger. Didn't look around. Just slipped out the back door like I was sneaking away from something sacred.

The air hit cold on my skin, sharp, like it knew what I'd just left behind. The night was still. Almost reverent. Like even the town was holding its breath, watching me go.

Free, maybe. But cracked in places no one could see.

Quiet, but echoing inside with everything I could never say.

Sue didn't ask any questions when I walked through the door that night. She looked at me, really looked at me, and nodded like she already knew.

I sat on the edge of our bed and held my boys in my arms for what felt like hours.

For the first time in years, I let myself fall apart.

No uniform, no rank, no pressure to be composed or in control.

Just me, raw wrecked, real.

I gave everything to this life, my time, my heart, my sense of self. In return, it gave me purpose, brotherhood and wounds I didn't recognize until long after they'd settled in.

But the truth was, I didn't know how to stop. I didn't know who I was without the chaos. Without the adrenaline.

Only now am I starting to understand.

That breathing isn't the same as living. That holding it all in doesn't make you strong, it just makes you sink quieter.

That walking away from police work isn't weakness.

Sometimes, it's the bravest damn thing you'll ever do.

Epilogue

I didn't stay gone for long.

Three months after I walked out the back door of the station, I signed on full-time as a firefighter in another city. Not because I healed. Not because I found peace. Because I didn't know how to be anything else.

Firefighting gave me purpose. A rhythm, a place where pain was expected and manageable, other people's pain, anyway. I told myself I was making a difference. Most days, I believed it. On the worst days, I just kept moving.

One call at a time.

The weight kept adding. Little by little. A child I couldn't save. A friend who didn't make it out. A hallway full of smoke that smelled just like Mara's garage. I buried them all in the same place, the quiet part of my mind where I swore, I'd deal with them later.

But later never came.

I became good at the job. Respected. Trusted. The guy who always kept his cool. No one saw how much I was cracking. Not even me.

It wasn't one call that finally broke something. It never is. It was a hundred. A thousand. A slow drip until something inside rusted through.

But that's a story for another time.

For now, I'm still out here, on the engine, in the turnout gear, wearing the weight like a second skin. Still showing up. Still carrying ghosts.

Somewhere out there, I know another call is coming, one I won't walk away from the same.

Again.

www.ingramcontent.com/pod-product-compliance
Lightning Source LLC
Chambersburg PA
CBHW070630030426
42337CB00020B/3968